AOC

★ ★ ★ ★ ★ ★

FIGHTER,
PHENOM,
CHANGE
MAKER

MS. OCASIO-CORTEZ

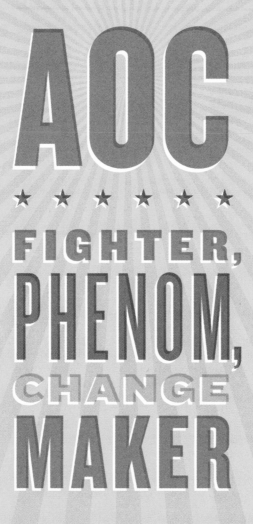

AOC

★ ★ ★ ★ ★ ★ ★

FIGHTER, PHENOM, CHANGE MAKER

PRACHI GUPTA

WORKMAN PUBLISHING
New York

For Dadaji

★ ★ ★ ★ ★

Library of Congress Cataloging-in-Publication Data is available.

ISBN 978-1-5235-1037-5

Design by Sarah Smith
Photo research by Kenneth Yu

Workman books are available at special discounts when purchased in bulk for
premiums and sales promotions as well as for fund-raising or educational use.
Special editions or book excerpts can also be created to specification. For details,
contact the Special Sales Director at the address below, or send an email to
specialmarkets@workman.com.

Workman Publishing Co., Inc.
225 Varick Street
New York, NY 10014-4381
workman.com

WORKMAN is a registered trademark of Workman Publishing Co., Inc.

Printed in the United States of America
First printing November 2019

10 9 8 7 6 5 4 3 2 1

CONTENTS

INTRODUCTION . . . . *vii*

PART ONE
A Girl from the Bronx 1
Two Zip Codes 2
Difficult Questions 11

PART TWO
Roots of a Movement 19
Paycheck to Paycheck 20
The Rise of Donald Trump 26
A Brand New Congress Awaits 34
Build Our Own House 42
We've Got People 54

PART THREE
Making History 63
Kingslayer 64
The AOC Effect 69
Women Win 74

PART FOUR
Political Rock Star 81
Meet the Squad 82
First, We Protest 85
A White Suit and Gold Hoops . 91
Social Media Queen 95
The "S" Word 103
Walking the Walk 107
Republican Obsession 113
Call Me a Radical 120
Moving Left 125

MAJOR PROPOSALS
Abolish ICE 128
Green New Deal 129
Medicare for All 130
Federal Jobs Guarantee 131
Free Public College 132

SOURCE LIST 133
CREDITS 134
ACKNOWLEDGMENTS 135

INTRODUCTION

ike many reporters across the country, after the 2016 election of Donald Trump, I reassessed my responsibilities as a journalist and reflected on what the media could have done differently. As an Indian-American woman covering the election in a landscape dominated by white people (mostly men), I had seen how, under the guise of objectivity, many mainstream media outlets humanized white supremacists and gave platforms to bigots; all the while, they policed the anger of people of color and struggled to call out racism by its name.

The months that followed the election clarified my purpose and my commitment to writing not just about, but also *for*, women of color—women who have grown up, as I did, not seeing our perspectives and experiences on TV or in the news. I wanted to write from a place that doesn't seek to justify or explain our humanity to others, but instead begins with the assertion that our experiences are valid.

It was with that renewed focus that I sought to write this book about Congresswoman Alexandria Ocasio-Cortez, a woman who embodies these values without apologizing or seeking permission. Ocasio-Cortez uses her platform to speak out against inequality where she sees it, regardless of party affiliation or political expediency. While she made history in 2018 as the youngest woman to be elected to Congress, she has also energized a national movement. Her message of economic and racial justice is one that resonates deeply with me as a millennial woman of color who graduated college during the Great Recession. It has been exciting to watch her and her fellow progressives work to push the country in a new direction.

PART ONE

A GIRL FROM THE BRONX

TWO ZIP CODES

When thinking about names for their first-born child, Sergio Ocasio suggested "Alexandria" to his wife, Blanca Ocasio-Cortez. "I thought about it for a while and I said: 'Alexandria Ocasio-Cortez. That sounds very powerful,'" Blanca recalled in an interview with the *Daily Mail*. "'That'll be her name.'" She gave birth to Alexandria on October 13, 1989. Twenty-nine years later, Blanca would stand beside her daughter at a ceremony on Capitol Hill, where she would witness Alexandria be sworn in as the youngest woman ever elected to Congress.

Alexandria Ocasio-Cortez and her mother stand with Speaker of the House Nancy Pelosi at the ceremonial swearing-in of the 116th Congress.

One of the buildings in the Parkchester community in the Bronx.

But the origins of Alexandria Ocasio-Cortez, now known around the world simply by her initials, "AOC," were humble: Her mother was a domestic worker from Puerto Rico, and her father, also of Puerto Rican descent, owned a small business in the Bronx, where the family lived in a condo in a planned community of 171 brick buildings called Parkchester.

The Bronx, New York City's northernmost borough, is the third most densely populated county in the country, home to 1.4 million people. It is incredibly diverse: More than half of its inhabitants are Hispanic or Latinx, and nearly half speak Spanish. Sergio grew up in the South Bronx when the county was gripped by a heroin epidemic and entire neighborhoods burned down in what remains the poorest congressional district in the United States.

Blanca, meanwhile, grew up in Puerto Rico, looking after her siblings while her mother worked to put food on the table. She met

Sergio on one of his visits to the island, where he had family. They married in a local church in Puerto Rico and then moved to New York City, where Blanca had to learn a new way of life. "My parents started from scratch: new languages, new life, new everything," Ocasio-Cortez wrote in a touching Instagram post celebrating her swearing-in to Congress. "Mami mopped floors, drove school buses, + answered phones. She did whatever she needed to do, for me."

★ ★ ★ ★ ★ ★ ★ ★ ★ ★ ★

In the early 1990s, the Bronx had the highest high school dropout rate of any county in the state. But Ocasio-Cortez's parents were adamant about creating more opportunities for their children. Sergio pooled money from relatives to buy a modest house about 30 miles north of the Bronx in Yorktown Heights, a more afflu-ent suburb, so they could give Alexandria and, later, her younger brother, Gabriel, access to better public schools. They moved when Alexandria was about five years old and Gabriel was a toddler.

"We had a great life there," Blanca told the *Daily Mail*. "Alexandria was very social, so she always had a bunch of girls over. She took over the shed in the backyard. She cleaned it up, put up curtains and photos and made it look nice, and that was like a clubhouse for her and her friends." Every year on their wedding anniversary, Sergio would spend the day roasting lechón in a pit in the backyard. On Thanksgiving, the family hosted neighbors, local employees, and others in the community who didn't have anywhere to go. "My dad used to say that he collected people," Ocasio-Cortez

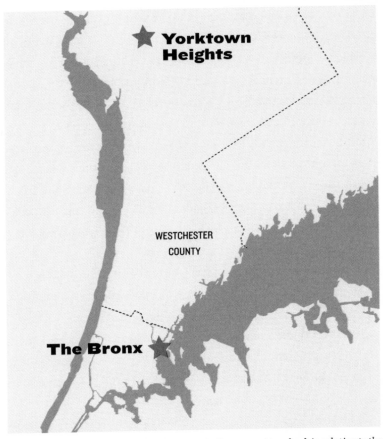

The location of Yorktown Heights, where Ocasio-Cortez went to school, in relation to the Bronx, where she was born.

told *Bon Appétit.* "If you didn't have a place to go on Thanksgiving, you came to our place."

During the week, the children attended school in Yorktown Heights, but they often returned to the Bronx, where Sergio ran his business and the kids were "essentially raised as siblings" with their cousins, Ocasio-Cortez told writer Ta-Nehisi Coates in 2019.

The Bronx was a different world, and the weighty contrast between the two neighborhoods exposed Ocasio-Cortez to the effects of income inequality at a young age. "That 40-minute drive, from where I went to school to where my family spent their time, kind of told the whole story," she told the *Intercept*. Calling for criminal justice reform in 2018, she wrote in the Jesuit magazine *America* about how "the webbed threads of poverty, geography, and lack of opportunity" swept up her cousin Marc and other men in her family "during the fever pitch of 1990s mass incarceration." In an interview with the *New Yorker*, she said that growing up, her cousins "were wearing T-shirts with pictures of their friends who had died—and that's just scraping the surface."

"I grew up with this reality and understanding of income inequality as, 'When I'm in this zip code I have these opportunities, and when I'm in that zip code I don't have these opportunities,'" she told Mic.com. "At a very young age I knew it was wrong. I knew that the fact that my cousins didn't have adequate resources or adequate public services and good schools, and I did, was something that just didn't strike me as right."

Living in Yorktown Heights enabled Ocasio-Cortez to nurture her intellectual curiosity at school. Blanca described her daughter as an avid reader throughout her childhood, and Ocasio-Cortez embraced her identity as a "dorky kid," telling *Time* that she once requested a microscope as a birthday present. Outside of school, Ocasio-Cortez was just as passionate about her studies. She traveled to Mount Sinai Medical Center in East Harlem to run science experiments, and at seventeen, she placed second in microbiology at the Intel International Science and Engineering Fair (ISEF),

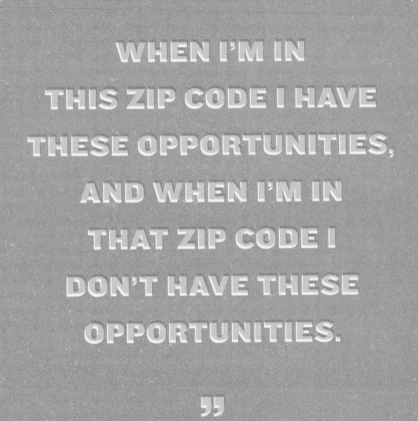

★ ★ ★ ★ ★ ★ ★ ★ ★ ★

"

WHEN I'M IN THIS ZIP CODE I HAVE THESE OPPORTUNITIES, AND WHEN I'M IN THAT ZIP CODE I DON'T HAVE THESE OPPORTUNITIES.

"

★ ★ ★ ★ ★ ★ ★ ★ ★ ★

the world's largest international precollege science competition. According to the organization that hosts the ISEF, her research on ringworms "indicated that antioxidants could potentially help prevent degenerative illnesses induced by oxidative stress." The MIT Lincoln Laboratory, which began naming asteroids for top students and teachers in science in 2001, named a small asteroid after her: 23238 Ocasio-Cortez.

It was also in high school that she got her first taste of politics: As a sophomore, she was selected to participate in the National Hispanic Institute's (NHI) competitive Lorenzo de Zavala Youth Legislative Session, an eight-day immersive leadership training program in which high schoolers engage in animated policy discussions, hold mock elections, and draft mock legislation. "She will tell you she ran for every position, she lost at everything," NHI official Julio Cotto said in a *Headliners* documentary, "but by the end of the week her peers had selected her as the most promising female of that delegation because they saw that never-quit attitude."

While she was excelling academically, Ocasio-Cortez was still

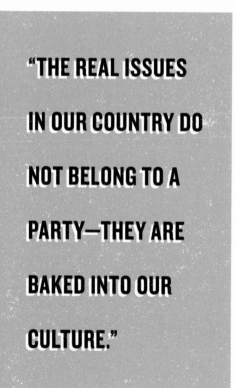

"THE REAL ISSUES IN OUR COUNTRY DO NOT BELONG TO A PARTY—THEY ARE BAKED INTO OUR CULTURE."

living in two worlds. "The thing that people don't realize is that wherever there is affluence, there's an underclass. There's a service class. And that's what I grew up in, scrubbing toilets with my mom," she told *Bon Appétit*. To pay for her after-school projects, she worked as a host at an Irish pub. In exchange for cleaning her home, one of Blanca's clients tutored Ocasio-Cortez for the SAT. Her college application essay, according to *Time*, was about helping a man grieving the loss of his wife by managing some of the small, everyday tasks that feel monumental during grief, like cleaning out his fridge.

She also received a lot of what she has called "subconscious cues" about race from her white classmates and the community at large: *Time* reported that she "told friends she learned early on that wearing hoop earrings and nameplate necklaces was fine in the Bronx, but she wouldn't be taken seriously if she wore them to a job interview." In an interview with Coates, Ocasio-Cortez, who went by the nickname "Sandy," talked about one incident in an AP Government class her senior year when she and her fellow students debated "whether English should be the mandatory first language of America."

"Someone was like, well, you know, if you're in America you need to speak 'American,'" she recalled. "This is in a liberal, affluent suburb." When Ocasio-Cortez said she learned Spanish as her first language, a girl shot back a doubly racist comment: "Well, you're not like *those* Mexicans."

"It was this real moment of consciousness," she told Coates, "that the real issues in our country do not belong to a party—they are baked into our culture."

In a 2017 Facebook post, she reflected on the complexity of Puerto Rican identity: "Indigenous DNA makes up a significant part of my genome. It co-mingles with the DNA of Spanish colonists who eliminated them from existence and the African slaves they replaced them with. Puerto Ricans clearly struggle with this in their broader culture, as they try to rediscover and maintain what little strands of indigenous and African culture may have been sneaked from ancestor to ancestor. Part of being Puerto Rican is to be all these things and none of them at the same time. It is to be something very old and something very new. It's still figuring that out."

Ocasio-Cortez's Bronx roots and Puerto Rican heritage undoubtedly shaped her sense of justice, identity, and moral clarity, which laid the foundation for her interest in policy and her eventual congressional bid. "She saw how unfair the system is, and she wants to change that," Blanca told the *Daily Mail*. "She saw struggling parents putting their children through school, but also how difficult life was for people in the Bronx compared to Yorktown Heights. She saw the difference in education and status between parts of the family, and she just wants everybody to have the same opportunities." Years later, when she took Capitol Hill by storm, she would proudly proclaim her identity as "a girl from the Bronx."

DIFFICULT QUESTIONS

y the time she was seventeen, Ocasio-Cortez had set her sights on pursuing a science-related career. She graduated from Yorktown High School in 2007 and attended Boston University, where she lived in pre-med housing and initially majored in biochemistry. In *We've Got People*, author Ryan Grim reports that Ocasio-Cortez registered as a Democrat the following January and was all in for Barack Obama, even phone-banking between classes and taking an overnight bus to New York in order to cast her ballot.

In 2008, she also secured an internship at the foreign affairs and immigration office of the late Massachusetts Senator Edward Kennedy. The experience introduced her to the brutality of the US Immigration and Customs Enforcement (ICE) agency, founded in 2003 to arrest, detain, and deport undocumented immigrants in the United States. "I was the only Spanish speaker, and as a result, as basically a kid . . . whenever a frantic call would come into the office because someone is looking for their husband because they have been snatched off the street by ICE, I was the one that had to pick up that phone," Ocasio-Cortez told Mic.com. "I was the one that had to help that person navigate that system." It was through

The Boston University East light rail station near BU's campus.

these heartbreaking first-person calls that she gained a deeper understanding of the challenges faced by undocumented immigrants and the horrors of ICE.

At the beginning of her sophomore year, tragedy struck. She told the *Intercept* that she was sitting in an economics class when her mother called to say that Sergio, who had been diagnosed with a rare form of lung cancer when she was sixteen, was not doing well. Ocasio-Cortez left campus immediately, flew back to New York, and visited her father in the hospital. Sergio Ocasio died on September 9, 2008. He was forty-eight.

"I didn't know that it was going to be the last time that I talked to my dad, but toward the end of our interaction, I started to feel like it was," she told *Time*. "I said goodbye, but I think he knew, and I knew. And so I started to leave, and he kind of hollered out, and I turned around in the doorframe, and he said, 'Hey, make me proud.'"

"My mother was *done*. My brother was *lost*," Ocasio-Cortez told the *New Yorker*. "I took it hard, too, but I channeled it into my studies. That's how I dealt with it." After taking only one week off from school, she took her father's last words to heart, and her grades jumped. "I come from a working-class background, so you don't really get a ton of time to mourn," she told the *Intercept*. Her father's death forced her to confront tough questions about legacy and mortality at a young age, she told Coates. "It really forced me to grapple with questions of . . . what do I want to do with my life?" By the time she would graduate from college and medical school and complete her residency, at least ten years would have passed, she reasoned, and even then she'd only be helping people on "a case-by-case basis." As she put it to Coates, "I wanted to examine issues on a more macro scale, which led me to start to study public health more."

★ ★ ★ ★ ★ ★ ★ ★ ★ ★ ★ ★ ★

During her junior year, Ocasio-Cortez studied in Niger for a semester, doing rotations at a maternity clinic on the outskirts of the capital city, Niamey. Niger has one of the highest rates of maternal death in the world, and in 2008, a woman's risk of dying due to pregnancy-related complications—most of which are avoidable with proper treatment—was one in seven. "I saw a lot of pretty brutal things there," she told *Bon Appétit*, including a grueling pregnancy that resulted in a stillbirth. "The reason the child had passed was very preventable. For me it was a very powerful moment." It reinforced a familiar lesson about inequality and opportunity: "This child's life was literally decided because of where it was born."

"I couldn't just go back home and lead a normal life," she said. Ocasio-Cortez's interest in public policy deepened, and she shifted her focus to economics and policy.

★ ★ ★ ★ ★ ★ ★ ★ ★ ★ ★ ★

Ocasio-Cortez became a leader in her college community and honed her public speaking skills. She cites former New York Senator Robert F. Kennedy, brother of Senator Edward Kennedy and former president John F. Kennedy, as one of her political heroes, telling the *New Yorker* that reading his speeches "was my jam" in college. She served as the president of Boston University's largest Latin American student organization, Alianza Latina, and as an ambassador at the Howard Thurman Center for Common Ground, a group committed to fostering diversity and inclusivity on campus.

Among her peers, she earned a reputation as an activist. "I didn't understand why people called me an activist," she told *Insider.* "I felt like I was just saying things that were very common sense. I would just say, 'Hey, kids in the Bronx should have a good education.' And they'd be, like, 'Oh, she's an activist.'"

In 2011, at a celebration honoring Martin Luther King Jr., a twenty-one-year-old Ocasio-Cortez delivered a speech to a crowd of about 300 students and professors with a slow, steady cadence. "Greatness has never been a result of circumstance or fortune," she said. "It is not an inherited trait or a function of destiny. Greatness dresses in humble clothes, emerging from tested integrity, unwavering belief, and unshakeable commitment. Greatness is the long haul. So I would like to respectfully defer the question 'Can we be great?' for perhaps a more pressing question: 'How can we be great?'"

King's ideas on justice were foundational to Ocasio-Cortez's moral vision and helped shape her platform in her eventual bid for Congress. He spoke against the inherent inequity in capitalism and called for economic justice in the form of democratic socialism, writing in 1966, "You can't talk about solving the economic problem of the Negro without talking about billions of dollars. You can't talk about ending slums without first saying profit must be taken out of slums. . . . Now this means that we are treading in difficult water, because it really means that we are saying that something is wrong with capitalism. There must be a better distribution of wealth, and maybe America must move toward a democratic socialism."

* * * * * * * * * * * *

But throughout her sophomore, junior, and senior years, Ocasio-Cortez's academic success and leadership were underscored by deep loss. Sergio's death was "destabilizing in every way," she told the *New Yorker*. Blanca barely staved off foreclosure and eviction. "It was difficult making ends meet," she told the *Daily Mail*. "I was skipping mortgage payments and we almost lost the house twice." On top of the financial hardship, Sergio did not have a will, landing the family in a protracted fight with the Westchester County Surrogate's Court.

His death plunged the family deeper into financial uncertainty at the height of the Great Recession, the longest period of economic

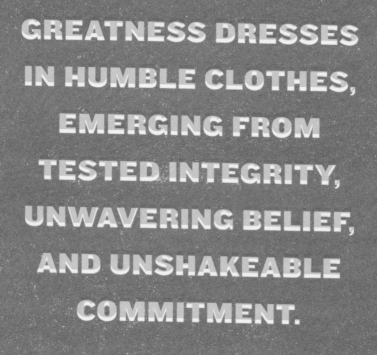

"

GREATNESS DRESSES
IN HUMBLE CLOTHES,
EMERGING FROM
TESTED INTEGRITY,
UNWAVERING BELIEF,
AND UNSHAKEABLE
COMMITMENT.

"

decline since the Great Depression of the 1930s. In the early 2000s, mortgage lenders began approving riskier loans, which banks bought in bulk with the goal of turning a quick profit. But soon, the market for these subprime mortgages dried up, and many of the big banks collapsed. Millions of people lost their homes; businesses shuttered. By 2009, the US unemployment rate soared to 10 percent, and more than 11 million people were without jobs.

Throughout college, Ocasio-Cortez had witnessed the corporate greed that fueled the financial crisis and watched taxpayers bail out Wall Street executives, who faced virtually no consequences. The recession deepened wealth inequality and it was the middle and lower classes, disproportionately communities of color like hers, that suffered most.

★ ★ ★ ★ ★ ★ ★ ★ ★ ★ ★

In 2011, at age twenty-one, Ocasio-Cortez graduated cum laude with a degree in economics and international relations and thousands of dollars in student debt, adding to her financial burden. Propelled by hardship, she quickly got to work to keep her family afloat.

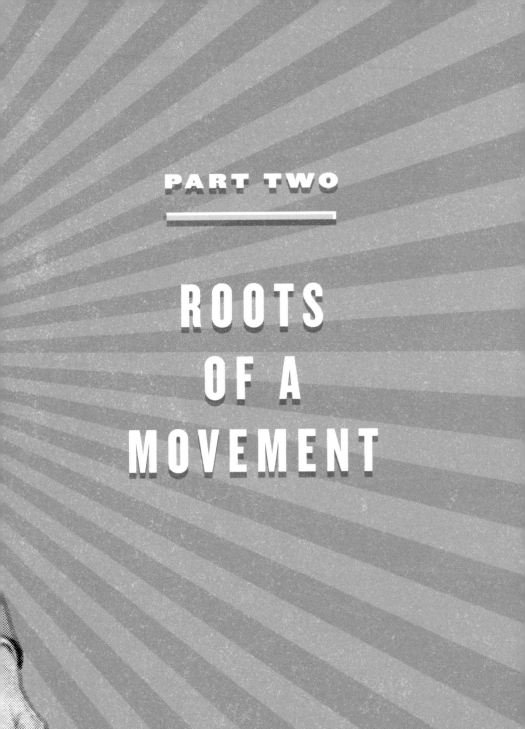

PART TWO

ROOTS
OF A
MOVEMENT

PAYCHECK TO PAYCHECK

By 2011, the economy was recovering, but barely. Across the country, there were still more than four unemployed people per job opening. Many recent college grads had amassed thousands of dollars of student debt and their job prospects were grim. "Our whole adolescence was shaped by war, was shaped by the increased erosion of our civil liberties and privacy rights, and then was shaped as soon as we got into college by a ground-shaking recession that has haunted our economic outcomes ever since," Ocasio-Cortez told *Insider*. "We have never seen an America where the fruits of capitalism have actually been good for an entire generation of millennials."

That year, she returned to the Bronx and entered the nonprofit world. She worked with the National Hispanic Institute as a social entrepreneur in residence and with the help of a local start-up incubator launched the now-defunct publishing company Brook Avenue Press. She envisioned bringing designers and writers together to create stories for children living in urban areas like the Bronx so they could see themselves reflected in art and the books they read. She also advocated for a bill cosponsored by New York

Senator Kirsten Gillibrand that would reduce business start-up costs, appearing at a 2012 press conference when Gillibrand introduced the bill.

But for most of her twenties, Ocasio-Cortez was living paycheck to paycheck, spending a large chunk of her monthly earnings on insurance and student loan debt. Money from her nonprofit work and entrepreneurial ventures was not enough to help her family stay afloat in the wake of her father's death, and she relied on restaurant gigs to make ends meet. "It was not long ago that our family's hope was so dim it was barely an ember," she wrote about that period of her life in an Instagram post. "Darkness taught me transformation cannot solely be an individual pursuit."

Ocasio-Cortez serves patrons from behind the bar.

The exterior of Coffee Shop, the restaurant and bar where Ocasio-Cortez worked.

Ocasio-Cortez began waiting tables at Coffee Shop, a now-shuttered restaurant and bar in Union Square, Manhattan, that *Eater* described as "a cultural sensation" due to its regular appearance on HBO's *Sex and the City* and the fact that it was operated by three former Wilhelmina models. She later tended bar at Flats Fix, a taqueria that the Coffee Shop owners opened around the corner in 2015.

Like a majority of women in the restaurant industry, she routinely experienced sexual harassment on the job. In his book *We've Got People*, Ryan Grim recounted one particularly disgusting incident in 2015: A manager ordered all of the servers to line up against the wall, including Ocasio-Cortez, and said that he was going to rate them on their attractiveness and give the best-looking staffers better tables. Ocasio-Cortez, whose campaign confirmed the incident occurred, was outraged and reportedly quit on the spot. According to the book, she agreed to stay only after management promised not to pull such a degrading stunt again. "What's wild is that I'm a member of Congress & I STILL found myself pausing at this, scared of possible repercussions of this story being public," Ocasio-Cortez tweeted after *Jezebel* blogged the account. "Imagine how everyday waitresses feel."

Eventually, she began to lose hope: "I was scrubbing tables + scooping candle wax after restaurant shifts & falling asleep on the subway ride home. I once got pickpocketed, & everything I earned that day was stolen," she wrote on Instagram. "That day I locked myself in a room and cried deep: I had nothing left to give, or to be. And that's when I started over. I honestly thought as a 28 year old waitress I was too late; that the train of my fulfilled potential had

★ ★ ★ ★ ★ ★ ★ ★ ★ ★

"

DARKNESS TAUGHT ME TRANSFORMATION CANNOT SOLELY BE AN INDIVIDUAL PURSUIT.

"

★ ★ ★ ★ ★ ★ ★ ★ ★ ★

left the station." Now she looks back and sees that time of despair as a new chapter of her life: "The funny thing about beginnings is that you rarely know you're in them. My beginning felt like a dead end," she wrote in an Instagram post in November 2017, months after she launched her bid to run for office. "My beginning was losing a parent to cancer, working a hard job in the wake of that loss, and complete uncertainty about the future of my family."

Ocasio-Cortez even credits working in the service industry as vital preparation for running her campaign. "People don't see waitresses as having a 'real job,'" she said in the documentary *Knock Down the House*, which followed the campaigns of four working-class women who ran for Congress in 2018. "But my experience in hospitality has prepared me so well for this race. I'm used to being on my feet eighteen hours a day. I'm used to receiving a lot of heat. I'm used to people trying to make me feel bad. They call it 'working class' for a reason. Because you are working nonstop."

 Alexandria Ocasio-Cortez ✔
@AOC

I find it revealing when people mock where I came from, & say they're going to "send me back to waitressing," as if that is bad or shameful.

It's as though they think being a member of Congress makes you intrinsically "better" than a waitress.

But our job is to serve, not rule.

12:20 PM · Mar 8, 2019 · Twitter for iPhone

THE RISE OF DONALD TRUMP

In April 2015, while Ocasio-Cortez was mixing margaritas, Vermont Senator Bernie Sanders, a longtime independent, launched an improbable bid for the Democratic nomination in the 2016 presidential election, vying to take the party in a new direction. His campaign rejected funding from super PACs—political action committees that allow corporations and unions to raise and spend unlimited funds to advocate for (or against) a political candidate. Instead, he funded his campaign mostly from contributions made by small-dollar donors, claiming to have raised an average of $27 per donor. He railed against the billionaire class and introduced radical proposals, like free college tuition.

Sanders immediately tapped into the anger of millennials like Ocasio-Cortez, who came of age during the Great Recession. His vision was inspiring: Within twenty-four hours of announcing his campaign, he had raised $1.5 million. By July, the self-described democratic socialist was attracting larger crowds than any other candidate running in the 2016 election. In December, *Time* magazine readers voted Sanders the "most important person of the year," placing him ahead of Malala Yousafzai, Pope Francis, and Barack Obama.

Among those "feeling the Bern" was Ocasio-Cortez. She volunteered with the Sanders campaign, knocking on doors in the Bronx and Queens as an organizer. In March 2016, she volunteered at Sanders's rally in the South Bronx, noting on her Facebook page that he was the first presidential candidate to campaign in the borough since Robert F. Kennedy in 1968. "I had done grassroots organizing before," she later told *Time*. "But Sanders's race was one of my first times where I crossed that bridge from grassroots community organizing to electoral organizing."

By the summer of 2016, Sanders had lost the Democratic nomination to Hillary Clinton. Donald Trump, a reality TV star and businessman who faced multiple sexual assault allegations, won the Republican Party's nomination.

As I mentioned in the introduction to this book, I covered the presidential election as a senior writer for Cosmopolitan.com. It seemed like a cruel irony that the man who first established his political base by demanding the first black president show his birth certificate would one day replace him in office, and it was a growing possibility that I, and many of my colleagues, did not want to face. Like most mainstream pollsters and political pundits, I believed that Clinton would pull through to win the general election, even if narrowly. As the election drew closer, several Republican commentators and voters who detested Trump's ideas told me they were braced for a come-to-Jesus moment in which they'd need to build, repair, and reassess the party's path forward. But on November 8, 2016, it was the Democratic Party that would split wide open.

Throughout the campaign, Clinton, a consummate politician, was not nearly as enticing for TV executives as Trump, who spoke in off-the-cuff platitudes and made controversial, incendiary comments. He was a ratings machine. Even supposedly neutral networks like CNN focused on Trump, enthusiastically running his speeches and unedited rallies. CNN president Jeff Zucker told *Vanity Fair* in 2018, "People say all the time, 'Oh, I don't want to talk about Trump, I've had too much Trump.' And yet at the end of the day, all they want to do is talk about Trump." As a result, Trump's hateful rhetoric received more airtime, and pundits began to debate his ideas, lending legitimacy to proposals like "a total and complete shutdown of Muslims entering the United States."

I watched in horror as his ideas embedded themselves into the American psyche. I thought about the media's role in enabling his rise, and wrote on Cosmopolitan.com that "I was struck by how, interview after interview on mainstream cable, statement after statement made by politicians, I saw almost exclusively white men and women in control of a conversation on issues that affect me and people who look like me." While I am not Muslim, I am a brown woman, and I know firsthand the sort of discrimination that such irresponsible rhetoric leads to. To me, televised debates about a border wall and a Muslim ban were not entertainment, they were erasure.

On election night, I was reporting at the Javits Center in midtown Manhattan, where Clinton's campaign expected to usher in America's first female president. As the hours wore on, it became more and more evident that there would be no celebration. Outside, I stifled back tears as I attempted to interview heartbroken Clinton supporters. I witnessed a local street vendor high-five a group of men, saying, "Hey guys, at least now it will be legal to grab pussy!"

I was hardly the only one to take Trump's words at face value: Across the board, women of color voted overwhelmingly in favor of Clinton, with CNN exit polls showing that 94 percent of black women supported the Democrat. Those polls found that white people, on the other hand, were the only racial group to vote in majority for Trump—including more than half of white women. Trump's rise laid bare to the country what I and so many women of color innately know: that racism and sexism are not abstract concepts or fodder for ratings, but ubiquitous, powerful forces that affect us daily in every facet of our lives. And so, while Trump's election was unexpected, to many women of color it was not exactly a shock.

But another important part of the election was who *didn't* turn out to vote. Although Clinton won the popular vote, more people chose to not vote than vote for either Trump or Clinton, according to a Pew Research Center analysis. Plus, a disproportionate share of

A crowd reacts as the results come in on election night in 2016.

nonvoters were people under thirty and people of color—groups that were more likely to support Clinton. White people, a group more likely to support Trump, made up nearly three-quarters of voters. In other words, as the *Washington Post* summed it up, "Nonvoters handed Trump the presidency." A crucial and early lesson that Ocasio-Cortez drew from the election was that while Trump had animated his base, Clinton had failed to build a movement that inspired Democrats. In a Facebook livestream in December 2016, Ocasio-Cortez opined on the loss, "It wasn't that people voted *for* Trump, it was that they didn't vote for Hillary."

★ ★ ★ ★ ★ ★ ★ ★ ★ ★ ★ ★

The next morning, New York City felt like a funeral. "I think so many New Yorkers remember the morning after the election because the election, of course, was on a Tuesday, and most of us had to go to work the next day," Ocasio-Cortez recalled to *Business Insider*. "It was so quiet on the subways, and we're talking about the train car was packed, absolutely packed with people, and you could just feel the heaviness on every single train car."

Overnight, the fates of so many immigrants, undocumented people, Muslims, LGBTQ+ people, and women—groups Trump had targeted in his campaign—were now uncertain. Once she was in office, Ocasio-Cortez said to *Vanity Fair*, "I'm gonna be very frank: I think that this president has set a racist tone. I think he has set a tone of such strong misogyny, racism, conspiracy theory-ism."

The atmosphere at Flats Fix changed: "So many of our immigrant coworkers decided to go back home to their home countries,"

Ocasio-Cortez at a protest in 2019.

Ocasio-Cortez said. People began "feeling like they weren't welcome in America anymore. And it has a real impact on our communities."

For Ocasio-Cortez, Trump's election was a call to action. The day after, she posted a surprisingly hopeful message on Facebook: "Social instability is a direct result of wealth inequality. And bigotry is a largely a result of poverty and scarcity. I know this may be hard to believe, but take refuge in the fact that sexism, racism, and xenophobia did not win last night. They were attendants to a larger stage. What won was the fight for struggling, working class people to be heard. And although I did not wish (nor vote) for this outcome, I at least seek to understand it."

That December, one month after Trump was elected, Ocasio-Cortez and two friends decided to take a road trip to the Midwest to get a "first-person idea of what was going on" in the country, she told *Mother Jones*. They raised about $1,000 via a GoFundMe page to deliver wood, wood-burning stoves, cots, subzero sleeping bags, and other essentials to the protesters who had set up camps near

An estimated 10,000 water protectors camp out at the Oceti Sakowin Camp in North Dakota.

the Dakota Access Pipeline and Standing Rock Sioux Reservation. Scott Starrett, a Flats Fix regular whom she had befriended, lent her a GoPro to document the journey and interview people along the way. They drove a 1998 Subaru, stopping in Flint, Michigan, to talk to people about the water crisis. Fueling themselves with Red Bull, Clif Bars, and Hot Cheetos, according to *Time*, they eventually reached the snowy plains of North Dakota, where they saw up close what Ocasio-Cortez called, in the *Mother Jones* interview, the take-over by "militarized corporations."

In July 2016, the federal government had approved a plan by Texas-based company Energy Transfer Partners to build a 1,172-mile-long oil pipeline that would bring 570,000 barrels of crude oil daily from North Dakota to Illinois. Called the Dakota Access Pipeline, it would cross under a Missouri River reservoir called Lake

Oahe, potentially endangering the main water supply of the Standing Rock Sioux Tribe. In the coming months, the Standing Rock reservation became the setting for a standoff between thousands of protesters, private guards, and law enforcement officials, building a national movement against the outsized power of corporations and the government's abuse of indigenous peoples and their land. Police blasted protesters with water cannons, rubber bullets, and percussion grenades in freezing temperatures, and in 2017, after the months-long standoff, police in riot gear and military fatigues cleared the camps to ensure completion of the pipeline.

In both Michigan and North Dakota, Ocasio-Cortez witnessed how the government suppressed the right to clean water in communities of color. She recognized that this could happen anywhere in the country, again solidifying the lesson from her childhood: that inequality is baked into our culture. Those experiences would later propel her advocacy for the Green New Deal, an activist-led package of racial, economic, and climate justice proposals to curb the damage of global warming and invest in underserved communities that have been disproportionately impacted by environmental disasters.

Slowly, a new goal came into focus: "I first started thinking about running for Congress, actually, at Standing Rock in North Dakota and South Dakota," Ocasio-Cortez said in a town hall on climate change led by Bernie Sanders after she was elected. "It was really from that crucible of activism where I saw people putting their lives on the line, and Native peoples putting everything they had on the line, not just for themselves," she said, "but for the entire water supply for the Midwest United States. . . . When I saw that, I knew that I had to do something more."

A BRAND NEW CONGRESS AWAITS

t the end of that trip to Standing Rock, Ocasio-Cortez received a serendipitous phone call. Some former Sanders staffers had started a grassroots group and were looking to train new candidates. They wanted to know: Was she interested in attempting a bid for Congress?

★ ★ ★ ★ ★ ★ ★ ★ ★ ★ ★ ★

In the middle of the 2016 primary, after they realized that Sanders was not going to win the Democratic nomination, several former Sanders staffers organized a PAC called Brand New Congress to recruit a new crop of diverse candidates who didn't have the money, status, or connections to get into politics. (Unlike super PACs, PACs cannot accept money from unions and corporations and face limitations on how much they can accept from a donor and give to a candidate.) In May 2016, Brand New Congress cofounder Saikat Chakrabarti announced on *The Rachel Maddow Show* that they were looking for candidates to tackle income inequality, money in politics, climate change, and mass incarceration.

The Ocasio-Cortez campaign calls voters to remind them of the upcoming election.

They received about 11,000 applications, one of which came from Gabriel Ocasio-Cortez—Alexandria's brother. He had nominated his sister as a candidate, and Ocasio-Cortez recalled to the *New Yorker* that her reaction was, "Eff it. Sure. Whatever."

The application caught the attention of the group. "We looked at the brother telling the story of a sister who wasn't a giant non-profit executive, she didn't go work on the Hill for 10 years," said Alexandra Rojas, executive director of Justice Democrats, a PAC closely aligned with Brand New Congress, in conversation with *Time*. "She was someone who watched her family struggle through the financial crisis."

Zeynab Day, communications director of Brand New Congress, told me that before reaching out to Ocasio-Cortez, they reviewed her social media and online presence. The group was impressed by Ocasio-Cortez's leadership abilities and how she translated politics into deeply personal, moral issues. "Immediately, we felt like she had an impressive spark."

Ocasio-Cortez, on the other hand, was less confident about her ability to run. Her opponent in the race would be ten-term Congressman Joseph Crowley. "I mean, I'm going to tell people that I, as a waitress, should be their next congresswoman?" she told the *New Yorker*, recalling her initial skepticism. Brand New Congress, along with Justice Democrats, began training and vetting nominees and then introduced Ocasio-Cortez to other recruits from across the country. But according to Virginia "Vigie" Ramos Rios, a former regional outreach and field director for the Sanders campaign who would eventually become her campaign manager, it would take until the end of April for Ocasio-Cortez to decide to go all in. Speaking at a political conference in Belgium in 2019, Ramos Rios said that some of the hesitancy "you could chalk up to being young, being a woman, having just seen what happened to Hillary Clinton in the presidential race." Explaining what changed Ocasio-Cortez's mind, Ramos Rios said the candidate asked herself: "If I'm not the one who will step in and do this, then who will?" Ramos Rios continued, "That was one of the most critical elements of her running, that she was running from a place of service."

* * * * * * * * * * * *

At fifty-six, Joseph Crowley was double Ocasio-Cortez's age and had held his seat in Congress since she was just nine years old. Crowley, the so-called King of Queens, was born in Woodside, Queens. His father was a Korean War veteran who, like his own

Joseph Crowley, Ocasio-Cortez's opponent, speaks in Congress in 2007.

father, became a New York City cop. Politics was in Crowley's blood: His uncle Walter briefly served as a city councilman, and his cousin Elizabeth served as a city councilwoman in Queens for nearly ten years. After graduating from Queens College in 1985, Crowley went straight into the family business.

In 1986, Crowley was elected to the New York State Assembly, where he would serve for more than ten years. Then, in 1998, he got a big break: Mere months ahead of a midterm election, seven-term Congressman Tom Manton announced his retirement. Manton secured the election for Crowley: He had already petitioned to get on the ballot, signaling a reelection bid, but at the last minute, he pulled out of the running. That late in the game, it's up to the Queens Democratic Party to pick another candidate. Incidentally, Manton also served as chairman of the Queens Democratic Party, so he essentially handpicked thirty-six-year-old assemblyman Joseph Crowley, the *New York Times* reported. Describing Crowley as Manton's political protégé, the *Times* wrote that Crowley came from a similar centrist mold: "Like Mr. Manton, he opposes abortion rights, supports tough anti-crime measures, including the death penalty, and takes a keen interest in Ireland."

Crowley eventually rose to the fourth-highest position in the House as the chairman of the Democratic Caucus and was rumored to be a possible replacement for Nancy Pelosi as Speaker of the House. Over time, he shifted further left on social issues, eventually supporting abortion rights (and earning a 100 percent rating from Planned Parenthood for his voting record) and supporting Medicare for all. But for much of his career, he was a centrist Democrat: He voted to repeal the 1933 Glass-Steagall Act, which loosened regulations on banks and contributed to the Great Recession. He voted for the Iraq War, supported the Patriot Act, and became one of the most prolific fund-raisers in the House, with strong backing from the real estate and financial industries and labor unions.

Within New York City, Crowley also served as the chair of the Queens Democratic Party, an all-powerful position that allowed him to control judicial appointments and determine how to fill vacancies in special elections. According to the *Times*, Crowley was "perhaps the last powerful party boss" in New York City, and "very little of consequence seemed to occur in Queens politics that Mr. Crowley or his cohorts did not have a hand in." In other words, Crowley wasn't just a politician—in New York, he was an institution. Crossing him was like crossing the Democratic Party itself. No one was supposed to challenge him, least of all an unknown, far-left twenty-eight-year-old who had no standing in politics.

But Crowley, a white Wall Street–backed politico whose family lives in his second home, near Washington, DC, appeared out of touch with the needs of his district, which is majority nonwhite and nearly 50 percent are immigrants. Yet before Ocasio-Cortez, Crowley had not faced a Democratic primary challenger since 2004. Ocasio-Cortez recognized that a bid against Crowley *had* to come from someone like her. "Anyone who wants to keep their job in New York City would never dream of challenging Joe Crowley," she said in *Knock Down the House*. "It has to come from outside of Queens, it has to come from someone who's new on the political scene that they don't foresee coming, that they can't offer a job or pressure in another way, and it has to be someone that represents our communities in more ways than one. Basically, an insurgent, outside, grassroots candidate that's a woman of color from the Bronx."

* * * * * * * * * * * *

In the 1930s, the Democratic Party aligned itself with the rising and powerful labor movement. President Franklin D. Roosevelt championed a series of economic reforms, financial regulations, and public programs called the New Deal to help rebuild the economy during the Great Depression. Following in the tradition of the New Deal, Democrats remained the dominant political party through the 1960s and brought with them a wave of progressive reforms that included the Civil Rights Act of 1964 and Medicare. But turmoil in the 1970s—a depressed economy, resentment over the Vietnam War, and backlash against the civil rights movement—ushered in a period of austerity and fractured the party. According to political scientists Joel Rogers and Thomas Ferguson, authors of *Right*

> "WHAT ANIMATES NONVOTERS IS FEELING LIKE SOMEONE IS REALLY FIGHTING FOR THEM."

Turn: The Decline of the Democrats and the Future of American Politics, the faulty lesson Democratic leaders took from the crushing loss to Ronald Reagan—whose administration gutted social welfare programs, abandoned civil rights, and passed tax legislation that exacerbated income inequality—was that the party must move to the right. By the 1980s, according to historian Lawrence Glickman, many high-profile Democrats abandoned the New Deal tradition, thinking that it was no longer relevant. Glickman called this "a fatal error" in the *Boston Review,* writing that "weakening and undermining their connection to government as an enabler of liberty helped normalize conservative political rhetoric." Many leaders in the party moderated their message to woo more swing voters and leaned into a corporate fund-raising strategy—which went hand-in-hand with centrism.

Many progressives blame the Democratic Party leadership's watered-down, centrist strategy for Trump's victory in the 2016 election. In *Autopsy: Democratic Party in Crisis,* a group of leftist activists and lawmakers examined Clinton's crippling defeat and concluded that the party's pro–working class message has "been undermined by its refusal to directly challenge corporate power, enabling Trump to masquerade as a champion of the people." The authors wrote that the "party's congressional leadership remain[s] bent on prioritizing the chase for elusive Republican voters over the Democratic base: especially people of color, young people and working-class voters overall." In an interview with the *Intercept*, Ocasio-Cortez echoed the same conclusions: "Our neglect of that is something we wholeheartedly have to take responsibility for, and correct for."

In July 2017, eight months after the stunning defeat, the Democratic Party was still scrambling to define its values and build a cohesive strategy. A *Washington Post*–ABC poll found that only 37 percent of adults in America believed the Democratic Party "stands for something," and 52 percent said the party "just stands against Trump." Even Crowley admitted that the party's message was unclear, telling the Associated Press: "That message is being worked on." But in the 2018 primary race, Crowley had positioned himself as the homegrown antidote to fellow Queens native Donald Trump, telling supporters, "I was born for this role."

To Ocasio-Cortez, opposing Trump was not a platform. As she posed to MSNBC the morning after her primary upset victory, "We have to stick to the message: What are we proposing to the American people? Not, 'What are we fighting against?'" She criticized the party's decades-old strategy of moderation: The Democratic establishment "thinks that running to the center, moderating our policies, being as close to a Saltine cracker as possible, is what's going to make us win elections . . . and I don't think that that's the case," Ocasio-Cortez said on *Pod Save America* months after her historic upset. "I think what animates nonvoters is feeling like someone is really fighting for them."

BUILD OUR OWN HOUSE

In early August of 2017, white nationalists and neo-Nazis, emboldened by the Trump administration, took over the streets of Charlottesville, Virginia, chanting "Jews will not replace us." That fall, Trump risked the fates of nearly 800,000 people with the announcement that he was ending Deferred Action for Childhood Arrivals (DACA), the Obama-era program that protected undocumented immigrants brought to the US as children. Soon after, the government failed to adequately respond to Puerto Rico, which was ravaged by Hurricane Maria, the worst natural disaster in US history. Trump had been in office for less than one year, and New York City's immigrant-heavy 14th District, which stretches across the East River and connects the eastern part of the Bronx with north-central Queens, was pulsating with a deep, raw energy that pushed back against his administration and its policies.

Ocasio-Cortez had kicked off her Democratic campaign bid back in May, but the necessary paperwork was mistakenly filed in the neighboring 15th District. The amendment to fix the error took two months to file, but in the meantime, she continued to campaign against Crowley. She knew she would have to find another way to reach voters to take on an incumbent who had the backing of the Queens Democratic machine.

"Lots of these folks were mad that I didn't ask for permission to run, that I also was not using the traditional structures of power in New York City to try to run," Ocasio-Cortez told *Refinery29* in June 2018, calling out the Democratic establishment. "I just started building this coalition and this power outside of the traditional system. In my opinion, if women and gender-expanding people want to run for office we can't knock on anybody's doors, we have to build our own house."

She held her first canvassing event in June 2017, about one year before the primary election, in Queens, and began speaking at rallies, meeting with activists, hosting town halls, and broadcasting her message on social media. "I spent the entire first part of this campaign just going to people's living rooms and having them invite their neighbors, and just doing little coffee parties for like six or seven months," she told the *New York Times*. "And that's how we really started this campaign." It was during one of these early events that she met Ramos Rios.

In September, local Queens activist and labor lawyer Ethan Felder invited Ocasio-Cortez to speak at a Queens Stands Together Rally in response to Charlottesville. Ocasio-Cortez introduced herself to a crowd of about one hundred people in MacDonald Park and made her case for why Democrats need to abandon centrism and adopt a stance rooted in social justice: "When times are dire like these," she said, "what is positive about them is that they offer times of great moral clarity . . . we know what the right side of history is." Citing Martin Luther King Jr., she continued, "In King's

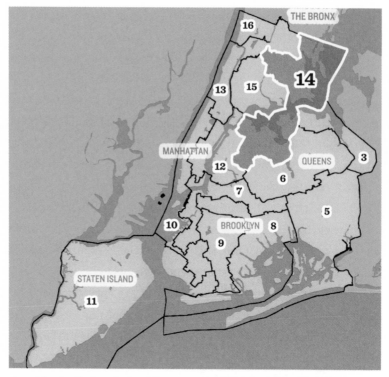

A map showing the boundaries of the congressional districts in New York City.

'Letter from a Birmingham Jail,' he discusses his grave disappointment with moderates, who are more devoted to order than to justice. . . . King's words are more important today, now more than ever."

It was in these early conversations and meetings that Ocasio-Cortez learned how to connect her vision and mission to the issues that people in her community cared about the most. "Folks were thinking that they were coming to listen to her, but she was going to listen to them," said Ramos Rios.

One of the core issues facing the immigrant-heavy district, Ocasio-Cortez realized, was the threat of ICE. That year, the administration quietly began separating migrant families at the US–Mexico border, paving the way for its new "zero tolerance" policy in 2018. Under the Trump administration, arrests of suspected undocumented immigrants were up by nearly 40 percent from 2016. "Things that were going on with ICE were things that were actually scaring them in their daily lives," Ramos Rios said. Immigrant activists had been calling to abolish ICE for more than a decade, and in early 2018, Ocasio-Cortez adopted the stance as a proposal in her campaign. Ramos Rios noted, "She was one of the very first people running for office to actually call for the abolition of ICE."

Despite her connection with crowds, in late 2017 Ocasio-Cortez's campaign was struggling. It's hard for a newcomer to gain any legitimacy without key endorsements, rich fund-raising networks, or traction in the polls—all of which feed off one another to build more power. As a political outsider, she had none of those things. Justice Democrats and Brand New Congress were stretched too thin to provide strong direction, so while Ocasio-Cortez was out "being a candidate," as Ramos Rios put it to me, for months the campaign and its handful of volunteers had no manager. Meanwhile, Ocasio-Cortez continued to work as a bartender four days a week. "For 80 percent of this campaign, I operated out of a paper grocery bag hidden behind that bar," she told *Bon Appétit*. "Between shifts at the restaurant, she'd reach into the bag for her political literature and a change of clothes, then set out to canvass," the magazine reported. She told Grim that in order to make more time to campaign, she started taking the express bus instead of the subway,

"

WE CAN'T KNOCK ON ANYBODY'S DOORS, WE HAVE TO BUILD OUR OWN HOUSE.

"

"which would take a little longer, but I could make phone calls and send emails and stuff on the ride."

By mid-February 2018, Ocasio-Cortez had saved enough money to quit her bartending job and focus on campaigning full-time. The team hired Ramos Rios to run the campaign. "The number one thing . . . especially in New York, is you have to get on the ballot," Ramos Rios told me. "That was the focus starting in February." She brought on the campaign's first staffers, and for the most part, they worked remotely or out of Ramos Rios's living room.

Though New York is a liberal state, its electoral process was notoriously outdated and cumbersome, which worked against challengers and suppressed voter turnout. According to a report by New York City's Board of Elections (BOE), while 62 percent of registered voters turned out for the 2016 general contest—slightly higher than the national turnout—a measly 8 percent of voters came out for the 2016 federal primary (the same contest Ocasio-Cortez would run in two years later). In addition to New York's draconian voter registration process, many people didn't even know there was a federal primary election in June 2018, let alone why such an election mattered. "There's so many people we were talking to who were like, 'Hey, I'm going to vote for the Democrat!'" Ramos Rios said. "It's like: Well, they're both Democrats."

Ocasio-Cortez needed 1,250 valid signatures from registered Democratic voters in her district in order to appear on the ballot against Crowley, but getting them was no easy feat. Most new candidates running in New York City have to collect far more than the required amount, because the BOE is notorious for tossing out signatures for minor inconsistencies. According to some of the arcane rules for collecting signatures, voters are required to sign the petition on the spot, and their addresses must match exactly what's in the files of the BOE (even if that data is wrong or outdated). A minor spelling discrepancy, or a "5" that looks like an "8," can render an entire signature invalid. These hurdles make it incredibly hard for a new, unknown, politically unconnected person to run—let alone run against one of the most powerful elected officials in the House.

Knowing that the BOE was stacked with Crowley's allies, the Ocasio-Cortez campaign originally planned to get 10,000 signatures—eight times the required amount. "In order to collect and produce that amount, you need a certain amount of campaign soldiers on the ground," explained Felder. In February 2018, Felder hosted a meeting at his apartment, where about two dozen activists and political organizers came to hear Ocasio-Cortez speak. "The folks in attendance at that party would form the small army that Alexandria assembled to get the petitions," said Felder, who joined the petitioning efforts. The campaign picked up volunteers at this house party and several others.

Ocasio-Cortez didn't have corporate money, but she did have a unique ability to tap into the growing activist momentum after the 2016 election and help people channel their energy into something larger than themselves. Between the end of February and early April about fifty volunteers braved cold temperatures (including three snowstorms) to petition for a candidate who was, in all likelihood, going to lose, even if she did manage to get on the ballot. "That gives you an idea of the fervency of people's beliefs in this campaign, in her movement, and in her as a candidate," Felder said. "It was a lot of grinding work, but you felt like you were part of a crusade." Meanwhile, the campaign used Crowley's complacency to its advantage and was careful not to advertise the petitioning effort. "We didn't want to trigger his sense of urgency or his spend," Ocasio-Cortez told the *New Yorker*.

In the opinion of Aaron Taube, field organizer for the Queens branch of Democratic Socialists of America (DSA) who joined the petitioning effort, one thing that establishment Democrats had underestimated was the surge in participation in local politics after Trump's election. "People had just accepted that because this machine had won for so long and hadn't really been challenged, you couldn't beat it. But I think what they weren't counting on was just [that] the number of people who paid attention to and cared about local politics skyrocketed after 2016," said Taube. Another motivating factor was ousting Crowley: "Queens was very activated based on the fact that Joe Crowley was the head of the County Committee, he's from Queens, and a lot of people in Queens felt under the thumb of the party," Ramos Rios told me.

Most of the volunteers were not seasoned in politics, but were a motley crew of "actors and bakers," said Taube, who led the Queens DSA's field organizing efforts after the DSA endorsed Ocasio-Cortez in late April 2018. "Everyone who worked in politics wouldn't touch our campaign with a ten-foot pole because of the fear of upsetting Joe Crowley and the Queens Machine. It was just all so many people who were doing this for the first time." Included in that core group were Naureen Akhter, a food blogger and cofounder of Muslims for Progress, who came on board as a neighborhood campaign captain; former actor Daniel Bonthius, who served as the spokesperson; and former theater lighting designer Jake DeGroot, who, in the final weeks of the campaign, created an innovative app that made it easier to keep track of voters. According to Ramos Rios, the campaign had up to 300 volunteers, 20 of whom were core members and about 100 of whom contributed regularly. The only criteria for volunteers were enthusiasm, commitment, and sharing in the campaign's common values.

★ ★ ★ ★ ★ ★ ★ ★ ★ ★ ★ ★

As soon as Flats Fix opened in 2015, Scott Starrett became a regular. He had befriended a bartender named Alexandria Ocasio-Cortez—or, as he knew her, Sandy. "Everyone just loved Sandy," he told *Insider*. "She had an infectious kindness, an infectious presence."

Ocasio-Cortez's campaign poster adorns a Bronx storefront.

Starrett's design firm, Tandem, would go on to create the memorable, brightly colored posters for Ocasio-Cortez's campaign about four months before the election. "We spent countless hours discussing politics with her before she began her bid, so we knew exactly where she stood on the issues, we knew the caliber of person she was and the style of campaign she was running, so it was a much easier challenge than most," he told *Fast Company*.

Crowley's campaign poster was uninspiring: a bland design using patriotic colors of red, white, and blue with a single message: "Re-elect Congressman Joe Crowley, Democrat." Ocasio-Cortez had been using Brand New Congress's generic logos, but in early 2018, she took a gamble on Tandem's design—it was riskier, yet more authentic. The posters did not blend in with their surroundings; the bold design immediately announced itself, attracting eyes to the diagonal typeface that danced across the poster. It prominently displayed Spanish alongside English, giving the two languages equal weight in a district where over 40 percent of adults speak Spanish, and also included the election date (June 26, 2018)—vital information for an election that wasn't on most people's radars. "We didn't want to slap the Spanish on and make these voters feel like they weren't part of the moment, because they are," Tandem designer Maria Arenas explained to *n+1* magazine. "You can also see it on the logo with the exclamation marks."

The Chavez poster that inspired designer Maria Arenas.

All of this was very much intentional, built around Ocasio-Cortez's identity and values, with a nod to civil rights icons from the past. "We're in a revolutionary moment, so we went straight to the history of grassroots, civil rights, and social justice movements in search of a common language we could participate in," Starrett explained. The designers found inspiration in labor leaders and civil rights activists Dolores Huerta and Cesar Chavez, cofounders of the National Farmworkers Association (now the United Farm Workers).

Arenas was struck by one Chavez poster in particular, in which the activist looks upward and to the right. Coincidentally, Ocasio-Cortez's friend and campaign photographer, Jesse Korman, had captured her at just the right moment, glancing upward to the sky.

It was important to Ocasio-Cortez to emphasize Spanish and multiculturalism not just on her posters but in all aspects of her campaign materials, including her website. In 2017, she told *Jezebel*, "Any person who wants to represent this district needs to *at least* be bilingual. . . . Not only is Spanish spoken here, but Bangla, Arabic, Mandarin, Albanian. . . . And I think that's really just representative of what leadership here needs to be." She continued: "There's no choice—if you want to reach the electorate, you have to do it in the language that the electorate speaks."

* * * * * * * * * * * *

In early April 2018, the Ocasio-Cortez campaign submitted approximately 5,400 signatures to the BOE. They were braced for a challenge from Crowley's camp, which could lock the campaign in court as BOE lawyers pored over the petition. Such a maneuver could have crippled the fledgling campaign, forcing it to divert resources to preserving a line on the ballot, even potentially blocking Ocasio-Cortez from appearing on it. But Crowley's campaign didn't challenge it. "At the moment, it looked like they didn't want to give Alexandria's campaign any more attention by challenging the signatures," Felder explained. Looking back, not challenging Ocasio-Cortez, he said, was likely "a strategic mistake on [Crowley's] part."

In early May, the BOE approved Ocasio-Cortez's petition: She was now on the ballot. "That was a real turning point for the campaign because it showed the wider political world and the grassroots world that this was serious," Felder said. That month, Ocasio-Cortez told the *Queens Chronicle*, "Regardless of the outcome, we've already made history."

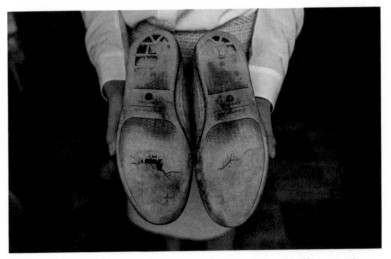

Ocasio-Cortez displays the shoes she wore for the first eight months of her campaign.

WE'VE GOT PEOPLE

fter Ocasio-Cortez got on the ballot, the campaign dialed up its get-out-the-vote efforts. As an incumbent, Crowley benefited from New York's traditionally low turnout at the primaries. On the flip side, that meant that Ocasio-Cortez had to meet a low threshold of votes to oust him. While Crowley was counting on continued support from his prime voters, Ocasio-Cortez sought to drive more people to the polls.

The nascent campaign opened its first office in Elmhurst, Queens, on May 29, just four weeks before the primary. It was a hot and humid day, and Ocasio-Cortez stood outside the office near the 7 train, where a crowd of about forty people gathered to hear her speak. "The 7 train is loud going by and she's giving her stump speech, getting everyone really roused. The microphone doesn't work properly, so she just throws the mic off of her lapel and starts speaking just off-the-cuff," Felder recalled. That moment "was kind of the epitome of the entire campaign," Felder said. "I was very skeptical of her chances," he admitted. "I didn't think that she would win on primary day."

Back in March, a Detroit-based filmmaker and member of the DSA named Naomi Burton reached out to Ocasio-Cortez on Twitter. "Her message was bold. It was unapologetic. It had a clear leftist vision that I could understand as just a normal person, that I thought other working people could identify with," Burton told the *Intercept*. "And after doing a little bit of digging, I realized she didn't have a campaign video." Burton, along with DSA member Nick Hayes, had founded a media production company, Means of Production, and were looking to support progressive, working-class candidates like Ocasio-Cortez. With a budget reportedly under $10,000, they filmed a two-minute campaign video with intimate shots of the candidate getting ready—putting on mascara, tying up her hair—at home in the Bronx, taking the subway, talking to local residents, and visiting her local bodega.

Ocasio-Cortez commutes to a campaign meeting.

"I was born in a place where your zip code determines your destiny," Ocasio-Cortez said in a voice-over. "I'm an educator, an organizer, a working-class New Yorker. . . . Going into politics wasn't in the plan. But after twenty years of the same representation, we have to ask: Who has New York been changing for?"

The video dropped on Twitter on May 30, 2018, and immediately went viral, racking up 300,000 views within twenty-four hours. "She sort of started taking off after that," said Zeynab Day.

Meanwhile, Crowley was less visible during the race. "Joe Crowley was interested more in Washington politics and less about his neighborhoods," Republican New York City Councilman Bob Holden told *City & State NY.* "I knew some people who lived in the area who said 'I got two visits from her campaign. I got a lot of literature from Joe Crowley but never a visit.'"

For Crowley, the primary was a speed bump on his road to Speaker of the House, and he mostly avoided his challenger. He didn't show up to the first debate with Ocasio-Cortez and even blew off another in-person debate, this time sending former city councilwoman Annabel Palma as a surrogate to represent his positions. Ocasio-Cortez highlighted the slight: "With all due respect," she said to Palma, "I'm the only one running for Congress in this room." On Twitter, Ocasio-Cortez noted that Palma, who is also Latina, bore "a slight resemblance to me"—the implication being that Crowley's choice of surrogate was racist.

When Crowley showed up to a televised debate on local outlet NY1 less than two weeks before the election, Ocasio-Cortez was ready. *Knock Down the House* captures Ocasio-Cortez preparing for the event, sitting in her living room and spreading her arms out

"

**THIS RACE IS ABOUT
PEOPLE VERSUS MONEY.
WE'VE GOT PEOPLE,
THEY'VE GOT MONEY. . . .
IT DOESN'T TAKE A
HUNDRED YEARS
TO DO THIS. IT TAKES
POLITICAL COURAGE.**

"

wide, reminding herself to "take up space" on stage and drive one point home: that she was fighting not for herself, but for a movement. She got her chance with a mic-drop moment: After Crowley said he'd support her if she won, he asked if she'd do the same. "Well, Representative Crowley," she replied, "I represent not just my campaign but a movement. I would be happy to take that question to our *movement* for a vote."

But by June 2018, Crowley had raised more than $3 million and received endorsements from heavyweights like New York Senator Kirsten Gillibrand, most local Democratic groups, and Planned Parenthood and the immigrant organization Make the Road. Meanwhile, Ocasio-Cortez had raised just about $300,000 and relied on endorsements from activist groups. But as the newcomer candidate put it to the *Intercept,* "You can't really beat big

Ocasio-Cortez waits to debate Joseph Crowley in Jackson Heights, Queens, in June 2018.

money with more money"; you need to "beat them with a totally different game."

Unlike Crowley, Ocasio-Cortez had refused corporate funds. She advocated for the abolition of ICE, a federal jobs guarantee, Medicare for all, and free public college, and she represented the working-class, immigrant roots that so much of the district came from. "It's so important for our community to see itself reflected in leadership. This could be the first time in a generation that the Bronx elects a new member of Congress—that's huge," Ocasio-Cortez told *Refinery29* ahead of the primary election. "And what we've shown is that you don't need access to money, to special social circles, to privilege in order to run for office. . . . If I win, imagine how many other people are going to do it."

* * * * * * * * * * * *

For most of the primary campaign, getting news coverage was difficult. "In Queens and even in the Bronx, a lot of the advertisers in the local papers are people who are tied up, in one way or another, [in] the various political parties. So even local coverage could be hard," Ramos Rios said. Ocasio-Cortez called out the mainstream media's bias toward powerful white male incumbents, summing up their failure to delve into her campaign with a poignant tweet referencing *Game of Thrones*: "A Girl Has No Name: Headlines from the Political Patriarchy." Instead, the campaign relied on coverage from progressive outlets like the *Young Turks* and the *Intercept*.

But Ocasio-Cortez was able to leverage technology and social media to amplify her message. As Grim reported, the campaign adopted a clever strategy from another Justice Democrats candidate, Jess King, whose Pennsylvania campaign targeted voters with digital ads on social media *before* ever knocking on their doors. That way, by the time a campaign volunteer arrived on a New Yorker's doorstep, Ocasio-Cortez wasn't a total stranger—they'd likely already seen her face and message on Facebook or Twitter. "What we did is load this [list of] 75,000 somewhat-likely primary voters into our digital marketing tools and we hit those folks with ads fairly frequently," Corbin Trent, Justice Democrats cofounder and former communications director for Ocasio-Cortez, told *City & State NY.* "Then we knocked on their doors, we sent them mail, we knocked on their doors again, we called them."

According to the *New Yorker*, the Ocasio-Cortez campaign made 170,000 phone calls, knocked on 120,000 doors, and sent just as many text messages to voters. "Regardless of what happens on June 26, we activated, trained and mobilized hundreds in a district that hadn't been mobilized before. That is permanent," Ocasio-Cortez said in an interview with *Huffington Post* that June.

★ ★ ★ ★ ★ ★ ★ ★ ★ ★ ★ ★

In an unexpected twist, less than two weeks before the primary election, California Representative Ro Khanna said he'd made a "mistake" in overlooking Ocasio-Cortez. In 2016, with support from the Justice Democrats, Khanna had ousted eight-term Democratic incumbent Mike Honda. But in the New York primary race, Khanna supported Crowley, explaining to the *Intercept* that "it is always very difficult for an incumbent to endorse a challenger to one of his colleagues." After facing backlash from progressives online, Khanna backtracked and issued a co-endorsement. "When I endorsed him, I did not look into Ocasio's campaign. That was my mistake. I should have been more aware of how inspiring a candidate she is and how she is a true trailblazer," he told the *Intercept*.

While the co-endorsement was embarrassing for Khanna, it was nonetheless a boon to the Ocasio-Cortez campaign. Khanna was the first and only member of Congress to endorse Ocasio-Cortez before the primary, lending her campaign legitimacy and putting it in the national spotlight just ahead of Election Day. "If Ro Khanna hadn't done what he did the way he did it, no way would that have got the attention it got," Trent told *City & State NY*.

★ ★ ★ ★ ★ ★ ★ ★ ★ ★ ★

That same month, the Department of Homeland Security revealed they had separated nearly 2,000 children from their parents at the US–Mexico border between April and May. Two days before the primary, Ocasio-Cortez took a break from campaigning to protest the administration's inhumane policies. "These are human rights abuses!" the candidate yelled, clutching a chain-link fence at a detention facility in the Texas desert. "I cannot sleep at night knowing these children are here." At the time, she was still a relatively unknown candidate. Three days later, the woman yelling at border officers through a fence would become a household name.

PART THREE

MAKING
HISTORY

KINGSLAYER

O n the day of the primary election in New York, *Jezebel*'s Ecleen Luzmila Caraballo visited Corona, Queens, and surveyed the scene: "The McDonald's I grew up getting hotcakes at had temporarily become a canvassing site. My elementary school had a stream of people flowing in and out of its doors during after-work hours, casting their ballots. And the Colombian bakery around the corner, which arguably sells the best coffee in New York, was the meeting spot for people eager to talk about what was happening around them in real time."

"I actually saw her campaign video on Facebook, and it just really resonated with me," one Ocasio-Cortez voter told *Jezebel*. "Because I come from a working family, and . . . I always thought that I was out of the ordinary, like I could never be in this spot."

"I think she's someone young and new," another voter said. "That's what we need. We need younger ideas, someone who is going to the office not expecting to be there for fifty years, who wants to get something done now."

Despite the buzz in Corona on that hot summer day, only 13 percent of the district turned up to vote. The day passed in a blur of anticipation, and after the polls closed at 9:00 p.m., *Knock Down the House* showed that, on the other end of the 14th District,

Ocasio-Cortez reacts after realizing she won the 2018 primary against incumbent Joseph Crowley.

Ocasio-Cortez was riding in a car alongside her mother, boyfriend, and others to a pool hall in the Bronx where her campaign staff, friends, and family had gathered to watch the results come in. She was too nervous to look at any of the reports and lingered outside, embracing her boyfriend, Riley Roberts, who comforted her: "Whatever happens, we did the best we could do." People inside began cheering and Ocasio-Cortez, sensing the excitement, screamed, "Oh my god!" Frazzled, she rushed past the bouncers, breathlessly yelling that she was the woman on the posters plastered all over the building. When she walked in around 9:40 p.m., she caught the first glimpse of the results on a large overhead TV: She was winning. An NY1 reporter waved a microphone in Ocasio-Cortez's face. Her expression was frozen in disbelief. "She's looking right at herself on television right now," the reporter said as

Ocasio-Cortez, mouth agape, remained speechless. "Can you put it into words?"

Ocasio-Cortez snapped to attention, swiveled her head, and exclaimed, "Nope!"

The photograph of this moment captures the surprise and excitement that swept the nation—Ocasio-Cortez had defeated the fourth-most-powerful Democrat in the House, a ten-term incumbent, by a margin of fifteen points, winning 57 percent of the vote in her district. She mounted the bar and delivered an impromptu, passionate speech to her supporters. "This evening changed America," she exclaimed. "This is not an end. This is a beginning, because the message that we sent the world tonight is that it's not okay to put donors before your community. The message we sent tonight is that . . . health care for every single person in America

A supporter and Ocasio-Cortez embrace after her win.

is what we deserve as a nation. What we proved tonight . . . [is] that there is still hope for this nation. That is what you have given this country."

She received congratulatory phone calls from Bernie Sanders and Hillary Clinton. Celebrities like Susan Sarandon, Chelsea Handler, and Ava DuVernay cheered for her online. "Ignore the women of color replacing the old guard at your own peril. Three words: Alexandria Ocasio-Cortez," DuVernay wrote on Twitter.

Upon seeing the results, Crowley conceded and played Bruce Springsteen's "Born to Run" on his guitar. He dedicated the song to Ocasio-Cortez. "It makes me emotional, just watching it, to handle that moment with such grace," Ocasio-Cortez said on CNN the next day. In a moment that revealed just how much of a political novice she was, she added that the two hadn't yet gotten ahold of each other because she couldn't find his personal number. "Yesterday, I was a constituent—and how do you find your congressman's phone number?"

In the days that followed, the media argued that Ocasio-Cortez won the immigrant-heavy district solely on the basis of demographics, dismissing the campaign's hustle. That narrative, according to a precinct-by-precinct analysis by the City University of New York's Center for Urban Research, is also inaccurate. Ocasio-Cortez had animated swaths of "drop-off voters"—people who don't typically turn out for midterms—and most of her votes came from areas that "were not predominantly Hispanic" and "are in the process of being gentrified," director Steven Romalewski told the *Intercept*. Ocasio-Cortez tweeted: "We won w/voters of all kinds. . . . We won bc we out-worked the competition. Period."

But that's not to say identity and demographics played no role in her victory. After Crowley reportedly criticized Ocasio-Cortez for being "unnecessarily divisive" and making the campaign "about race," she rebutted in the *Intercept*: "It is about race. . . . And it is about wealth inequality. Because this campaign is about our issues." Ocasio-Cortez's identity as a Latina from the Bronx helped shape her understanding of inequality, resulting in an ability to understand the needs of the people in her district and translate those into a platform that better represented them. Her campaign and the platform she fought for were inspiring to her volunteers and voters partly *because* they were so firmly rooted in her identity and personal history.

Overnight, Ocasio-Cortez went from obscurity to *The Late Show with Stephen Colbert*, where she dug into the president, saying, "I don't think he knows how to deal with a girl from the Bronx." The audience roared.

Ocasio-Cortez appears on The Late Show with Stephen Colbert *the day after her primary win.*

THE AOC EFFECT

hen she met the *New Yorker*'s David Remnick for dinner the Sunday after the primary, Ocasio-Cortez was greeted as a "local celebrity," he wrote.

"You're speaking to me when I am still emotionally, intellectually, spiritually, and logistically processing all of this," she told Remnick. "The whole thing's got me knocked a little flat."

Many people have found it difficult to combat the increasing sense of helplessness and fatigue associated with the onslaught of depressing headlines ever since Trump took office. Ocasio-Cortez's primary win cut through that darkness. Progressives and activists embraced her as a kingslayer who had, by dethroning a powerful white congressman, suddenly made the impossible seem possible. If a young Latina bartender from the Bronx could beat the establishment, what was stopping anyone else? Reporters hastily began searching for the next political upset, positioning candidates like Massachusetts's Ayanna Pressley, who ran against ten-term Congressman Mike Capuano, as "the next Alexandria Ocasio-Cortez."

In the remaining months until the general election in November, Ocasio-Cortez campaigned alongside Bernie Sanders and endorsed progressive candidates in races across the country.

Ocasio-Cortez speaks alongside Senator Bernie Sanders during a press conference to introduce college affordability legislation in 2019.

Cori Bush, a nurse and minister who made a congressional bid in St. Louis, Missouri, told the *New Yorker* that donations spiked from $9 to $2,000 in one day. Brent Welder, a labor attorney and former Sanders campaign organizer running for Congress in Kansas, told the *Huffington Post* that support from Ocasio-Cortez tripled his donations from $17,000 to more than $56,000. DSA membership soared to a record high, with sign-ups surging by thirty-five times the daily average the day after the primary election, and the Merriam-Webster online dictionary reported a sharp increase in searches for "socialism" that same day. Ocasio-Cortez's lipstick, Stila liquid matte in the shade "Beso," reportedly sold out on Stila's and Sephora's websites in June 2018.

It was clear that a movement was afoot, but the boost didn't exactly translate into a crashing wave of radical reform: Of all the candidates that Brand New Congress and Justice Democrats recruited in 2018, Ocasio-Cortez was the only one elected to office in November.

The Democratic Party's leadership has been less than enthusiastic about clearing the path for insurgent progressive candidates. Responding to the increasing influence of PACs like Justice Democrats and Brand New Congress, in March 2019 the Democratic Congressional Campaign Committee (the party's powerful fund-raising arm) blacklisted firms that worked with candidates challenging Democratic incumbents.

Monica Klein, a political strategist who has worked on campaigns for Ocasio-Cortez–backed candidates like Queens public defender Tiffany Cabán and State Senator Jessica Ramos in New York City, explained in the *Intercept* that while Ocasio-Cortez's success has inspired challengers, Democratic Party fund-raisers still overwhelmingly support "the heavily white, male incumbent Democrats in Washington."

Saikat Chakrabarti, Ocasio-Cortez's former chief of staff and Justice Democrats cofounder, told *Rolling Stone* that despite the losses by their other recruits, there's another way to measure success: "We're OK losing 90 percent of our races, if it means that the ones we win cause the kind of shift in thinking about what's possible—like Alexandria's race honestly did."

That summer, Ocasio-Cortez visited the Capitol and reflected on her wild, unexpected trajectory and the forces that propelled her onto this journey. She reminisced about a childhood road trip she

Alexandria Ocasio-Cortez ✓
@AOC

I have been getting many inquiries about my debate lip
color in the last two days.

I GOT YOU.

It's Stila "Stay All Day" Liquid in Beso. 💄

12:45 PM · Jun 17, 2018 · Twitter for iPhone

On Twitter, Ocasio-Cortez reveals the brand and shade of lipstick she wore to a debate.

took with her dad and his three friends, after she begged him to let her join, and a stop they made at the reflecting pool in front of the Washington Monument. "My dad pointed to all of it—the reflecting pool, the monuments, the Capitol," she told Remnick, "and he said, 'You know, this is *our* government. All of this belongs to us. It belongs to you.'

"And so, when I went to the Capitol, I thought about that," she continued. "I feel like it's *supposed* to belong to us. Not all of it belongs to all of us. Not yet. But that's the whole point of going to Congress, isn't it?"

A view of the Lincoln Memorial Reflecting Pool, which Ocasio-Cortez visited with her dad.

WOMEN WIN

espite her initial victory, there was still another race to win. The November 2018 general election pitted Ocasio-Cortez against Republican Anthony Pappas, a seventy-two-year-old associate professor of economics at St. John's University who had run unopposed in the primary.

His campaign seemed to revolve around his bitter divorce, in which he owed $1.5 million in court settlements to his ex-wife (court documents show that Pappas's ex-wife had a twenty-year restraining order against him and that he had allegedly punched her in the face). He denied the allegations and said in an interview with WNYC that the judges had gone "overboard" in imposing restraining orders and freezing his bank accounts. He sued the judges and explained, "I'm trying to expose this and reform it and help thousands of people that are suffering from an unaccountable judicial system," he said.

Pappas posed no threat to Ocasio-Cortez's candidacy— registered Democrats outnumber Republicans by almost six to one in the 14th District. He was also the only person who wanted to run in a race that everyone assumed would be pointless because of Crowley's dominance. "He had a very good pedigree on paper," Queens GOP Chairwoman Joann Ariola told WNYC. He earned unanimous endorsements from the GOP of both the Bronx and Queens. But apparently, Pappas had not shared details about the domestic violence allegations or his gripe with judges when he sought support from the GOP organizations. "Had he shared that with us ahead of time he would never have received the endorsement," Ariola told WNYC.

After Ocasio-Cortez won the primary, the local Republican Party wanted to put a more compelling candidate on the ballot. They couldn't, however, because Pappas refused to step aside or run in a different race. "It puts us in a terrible position where we could have won this election and now we have a candidate who we honestly cannot be proud of," Ariola told the outlet. The party was forced to continue with Pappas. But at the last minute, there was one more hiccup. Joseph Crowley was somehow still on the ballot. How could that be possible?

Ahead of the primaries, Crowley had received an endorsement from the progressive Working Families Party (WFP), a group of labor unions and activists that had also backed actress Cynthia Nixon in her gubernatorial bid against New York Governor Andrew Cuomo. As a minor political party, the WFP has a line on ballots in several states, alongside Democratic Party and Republican Party candidates. Although they can put forth their own candidates, oftentimes the WFP endorses a major party candidate who aligns with their values and interests. After Ocasio-Cortez's upset, the party backed her and asked Crowley's campaign to vacate the line. Although Crowley had conceded to Ocasio-Cortez

"

MY DAD POINTED
TO ALL OF IT—
THE REFLECTING POOL,
THE MONUMENTS,
THE CAPITOL, AND HE SAID,
'YOU KNOW, THIS IS *OUR*
GOVERNMENT. ALL OF
THIS BELONGS TO US.
IT BELONGS TO YOU.'

"

and vowed not to campaign, he reportedly declined to vacate the ballot.

"You'd think that given the moment we're in," Bill Lipton, the state director of the WFP, told the *New York Times*, "that Democratic leaders would want to help progressive forces to unite." But New York's byzantine election rules made it unexpectedly complicated to withdraw Crowley's name: Crowley would have had to run for a different position (one that he did not necessarily want or have a shot at winning), register to vote in a different state, commit a felony, or die. Ocasio-Cortez and Crowley sparred over the ballot on Twitter, with Ocasio-Cortez accusing Crowley of supporting her candidacy in name only. But in the end, Crowley's appearance on the ballot did not alter the outcome of the election. On November 6, 2018, the day of the general election, Ocasio-Cortez won by a landslide with 78 percent of the vote, trouncing Pappas, who earned 14 percent. Crowley won less than half of Pappas's votes, coming in at 6.6 percent.

★ ★ ★ ★ ★ ★ ★ ★ ★ ★ ★ ★

That same day, several candidates—many supported by Ocasio-Cortez—ousted most of New York's conservative bloc of Democratic legislators. For the first time since 2010, Democrats took control of the State Senate and quickly passed a series of reforms that had been stalled for years, like the Reproductive Health Act, which codified *Roe v. Wade*, and electoral reform that brought early voting to the state.

It wasn't just New York that made progressive strides. Nevada ushered in an all-female state legislature—the first in the country. Kansas's Sharice Davids and New Mexico's Deb Haaland became the first Native American women in Congress (Davids, who is openly gay, also made history as the first LGBTQ+ member of the state's congressional delegation). Minnesota's Ilhan Omar, a Somali-American refugee, and Michigan's Rashida Tlaib, a Palestinian-American, became the first Muslim women elected to Congress. Massachusetts elected its first black congresswoman, Ayanna Pressley. A record number of 117 women (100 of them Democrats) were elected or appointed to office, 42 of whom were women of color, and at least 3 identified as LGBTQ+. Democrats earned forty seats in the House, giving them the largest Democratic House gain since 1974. The victors formed the most diverse Congress in US history, and, two years after Trump rode into the White House on a wave of white nationalism, the freshman class became a beacon of hope.

While the 2018 midterms were inspiring, the numbers also reflect how far America needs to go until women have equal representation in government. Women make up more than half the population, but they hold less than a quarter of the seats in the House. At the current rate, it will take about one hundred years until women achieve parity in Congress. Meanwhile, white men, who make up 30 percent of the population, hold more than 60 percent of elected offices across the country.

But there is a slim silver lining: "We found women of color, white women, and men of color win at essentially the same rate," Reflective Democracy Campaign Director Brenda Choresi Carter

An image from photographer Martin Schoeller's Vanity Fair *spread in early 2019 (from left: Ocasio-Cortez, Ayanna Pressley, Ilhan Omar, Deb Haaland, Veronica Escobar, Sharice Davids).*

told reporters on a press call for the group's report on the 2018 midterm elections. "While white men still hold a monopoly on political power, they definitely do not hold a monopoly on electability." When more women run, more women win.

PART FOUR

POLITICAL
ROCK STAR

MEET THE SQUAD

O ne week after the general election, the freshman class of the 116th Congress convened in Washington, DC, for the first day of orientation. Among them were Rashida Tlaib; Ilhan Omar; Ayanna Pressley; and, of course, Ocasio-Cortez.

Collectively, in the halls of Congress, they became a force that represented what the future of the Democratic Party could look like—black and brown, female, unapologetic, and ultra-progressive. A *New Yorker* cover by Barry Blitt put a sharper point on it, depicting Ocasio-Cortez and her fellow progressives in colorful illustrations, bursting into a room full of monochromatic men. They appeared like a crew of new superheroes, defending America against an army of balding white men.

Cartoonist and illustrator Barry Blitt's depiction of Ocasio-Cortez and fellow freshmen on the November 19, 2018 cover of the New Yorker.

Ocasio-Cortez, Pressley, and Tlaib smile at a House Committee on Oversight and Reform meeting in April 2019.

The media covered the new class like superstars. The March 2019 *Rolling Stone* cover featured Connecticut Representative Jahana Hayes, Ilhan Omar, and Ocasio-Cortez alongside Speaker of the House Nancy Pelosi with the title: "Women shaping the future." *Vanity Fair* published a photo spread with Ocasio-Cortez and other freshman congresswomen, of whom photographer Martin Schoeller said, "They're very open, even free to dance in front of the camera, which I truly have never experienced before. They were so different from all the politicians I've met in the past, and they don't look like the sculptures you see in the rotunda, either." Though they weren't afraid to dance, they also recognized the weight of the moment. As Omar put it in one photo caption, "We did not come to play."

These women were on a mission to give Americans universal health care, to end the deportation of immigrants, and to call out corporate influence, racism, sexism, and xenophobia wherever they saw it—even within their own party. Their politics, inextricably linked to their identities, created a tiny ripple of change, perhaps the first in a tsunami of transformation coming for Congress.

Ocasio-Cortez and Omar arrive at the East Front of the Capitol in January 2019.

FIRST, WE PROTEST

On the first day of orientation, 150 protesters from the youth-led climate-change activist group Sunrise Movement and Justice Democrats gathered outside Nancy Pelosi's office. They were there to demand immediate action on climate change in the form of the Green New Deal, an ambitious set of economic, justice, and environmental proposals designed to combat climate change, boost the economy, and reduce the racial disparity wrought by climate-related disasters.

They had reached out to Ocasio-Cortez for support, hoping for at least a tweet. Instead, the congresswoman-elect showed up at Pelosi's office and joined them in their protest. "We need a Green New Deal and we need to get to one hundred percent renewables, because our lives depend on it," Ocasio-Cortez told reporters. "I—not just as an elected member, but as a twenty-nine-year-old woman—am thinking not just about what we are going to accomplish in the next two years but the America that we're going to live in in the next thirty years."

Facing public pressure from the activists and Ocasio-Cortez, Pelosi established the House Select Committee for the Climate Crisis in January, but the group doesn't have the power to subpoena witnesses or documents, and it permits lawmakers who receive fossil fuel money to serve on the committee, allowing for a

Ocasio-Cortez speaks to Sunrise Movement activists at the protest outside Pelosi's office.

potential conflict of interest. Ocasio-Cortez declined Pelosi's invitation to join the committee and instead introduced a Green New Deal resolution with Massachusetts Senator Edward Markey.

★ ★ ★ ★ ★ ★ ★ ★ ★ ★ ★ ★

In December 2018, freshman progressives protested corporate influence in politics at a bipartisan orientation for newly elected representatives, hosted by the Harvard Institute of Politics. The conference was cosponsored by two conservative think tanks, and speakers included General Motors chairman and CEO Mary Barra, Johnson & Johnson chairman and CEO Alex Gorsky, and Secretary of Transportation Elaine Chao (who, in June 2019, was under investigation for allegedly diverting agency funds to help her husband, Republican Senate Majority Leader Mitch McConnell).

On the first evening, rather than listening to Chao's welcome remarks, Ocasio-Cortez, Pressley, and other newly elected Democrats held a press conference of their own to advocate for single-payer health care, gun control, and urgent action on climate change. "We refuse to put hope and aspiration and values on a shelf," said Pressley at the rally.

When Gary Cohn, former chief economic adviser to Trump and former Goldman Sachs CEO, told the freshman lawmakers that they "don't know how the game is played" in Washington, Tlaib tweeted, "No Gary, YOU don't know what's coming - a revolutionary Congress that puts people over profits."

Over the next couple days, Ocasio-Cortez continued to document the orientation on social media, giving her followers a candid, behind-the-scenes look into how power is created and vested in Congress. In her tweets and stories, she criticized the heavy influence of executives over workers:

Alexandria Ocasio-Cortez ✔ @AOC · Dec 6, 2018
Right now Freshman members of Congress are at a "Bipartisan" orientation w/ briefings on issues.

Invited panelists offer insights to inform new Congressmembers' views as they prepare to legislate.

# of Corporate CEOs we've listened to here: 4
# of Labor leaders: 0

Ocasio-Cortez has received criticism from her party for speaking out against its leaders and explained why she pushes back in an Instagram post: "'Go protest Republicans,' we were told. 'You're being disruptive and unhelpful,' we were admonished. But the thing about protesting Republicans is that none of them listen." Referencing the October 2018 confirmation hearing of Supreme Court Justice Brett Kavanaugh, which Republicans manipulated and rushed through despite allegations of sexual misconduct, Ocasio-Cortez continued, "We learned that w/ the Kavanaugh fight and so many before that. Democrats, on the other hand, DO listen. So when everyday people show up in numbers and ask for change with commitment and consistency, we can get somewhere. And we are."

★ ★ ★ ★ ★ ★ ★ ★ ★ ★ ★ ★

Two weeks before she was sworn in, the millennial lawmaker made a surprising announcement: She was disappearing from public life. (Well, sort of.) "I am taking the week off and taking care of me," she wrote in an Instagram story in late December.

In recent years, the concept of self-care has been watered down to a buzzword that advertisers use to sell everything from pricey facials to temporary tattoos to tea. Flipping through a women's magazine or browsing wellness websites, it's easy to get the impression that self-care is a hot new trend among privileged white women. But self-care is rooted in the medical and mental health communities. In the 1960s, it became a tool used by civil rights leaders to take control of and prioritize the health of women and people of color in a society where they faced disproportionately

Ocasio-Cortez speaks at the rally outside the orientation for newly elected representatives at Harvard University.

higher rates of poverty and harassment and had less access to health care. As historian Natalia Mehlman Petrzela, an assistant professor at the New School, told *Slate*, self-care became "a claiming [of] autonomy over the body as a political act against institutional, technocratic, very racist, and sexist medicine."

Ocasio-Cortez, who had developed a loyal following, opened up about her disorienting adjustment to celebrity with an admission that was refreshing and humanizing. "I went from doing yoga and making wild rice and salmon dinners to eating fast food for dinner and falling asleep in my jeans and makeup," she wrote. "We live in a culture where that kind of lifestyle is subtly celebrated as 'working hard,' but I will be the first to tell you it's NOT CUTE and makes your life harder on the other end."

She also called attention to self-care's radical roots, reminding her followers that activists and leaders need to make time for their health in order to avoid burnout. She also posted a link to Amnesty International's self-care tips. "I keep things raw and honest on here since I believe public servants do a disservice to our communities by pretending to be perfect. It makes things harder for others who aspire to run someday if they think they have to be superhuman before they even try." For the next several days, Ocasio-Cortez laid low. And then it was time to get to work.

A WHITE SUIT AND GOLD HOOPS

O n January 3, 2019, wearing a white suit, large gold hoop earrings, and her signature cherry-red lipstick, Alexandria Ocasio-Cortez placed her left hand on a Bible and took an oath to support the Constitution of the United States. Standing among family, including her mother,

Surrounded by her family and friends, Ocasio-Cortez prepares for the opening session of the 116th Congress.

Ocasio-Cortez at the first session of the 116th Congress.

her brother, and her boyfriend, Ocasio-Cortez, twenty-nine, was sworn in to the 116th Congress.

She commemorated the moment by paying tribute to those who came before her. The suit represented the white that suffragettes wore when fighting for the right to vote at the turn of the last century and the white that women elected into office before her have also worn. Among those women was Shirley Chisholm, the Brooklyn public school teacher who made history in 1968 by becoming America's first black woman elected to Congress. "Fighting Shirley," as she was known, served for fourteen years, and she made history again in 1972, when she became the first black woman to seek the presidential nomination of a major party.

Ocasio-Cortez has paid tribute to Chisholm numerous times, including taking a picture of herself in front of Chisholm's portrait, which she shared on Instagram and Twitter in

Alexandria Ocasio-Cortez ✓
@AOC

♥

4:33 PM · Nov 30, 2018 · Twitter for iPhone

Ocasio-Cortez poses for a photo with a portrait of Shirley Chisholm,
America's first black woman elected to Congress.

November 2018. In a post about the inauguration, she wrote, "From suffragettes to Shirley Chisholm, I wouldn't be here if it wasn't for the mothers of the movement."

Ocasio-Cortez's earrings and lipstick were a nod to her Bronx roots and to liberal Supreme Court Justice Sonia Sotomayor, the first Latina justice, who, like Ocasio-Cortez, hails from a Puerto

Shirley Chisholm, one of Ocasio-Cortez's inspirations, sits with fellow members of the Congressional Black Caucus in 1971.

Rican family from the Bronx. "Lip+hoops were inspired by Sonia Sotomayor, who was advised to wear neutral-colored nail polish to her confirmation hearings to avoid scrutiny. She kept her red," she wrote in a tweet. "Next time someone tells Bronx girls to take off their hoops, they can just say they're dressing like a Congresswoman."

In an Instagram post thanking her mother for her sacrifices, Ocasio-Cortez reflected on the emotional moment. "This week I was sworn in as the youngest woman in American history to serve in the United States Congress. I hope that record is broken again soon. As I raised my hand for the oath, my mother held the holy book & looked into @SpeakerPelosi's eyes," she wrote. "Afterwards, the Speaker said to her 'you must be so proud,' and my mother began to cry."

SOCIAL MEDIA
QUEEN

The celebration, however, was short-lived: When Ocasio-Cortez joined Congress in early 2019, the country was stuck in the middle of the longest government shutdown in US history, during which an estimated 800,000 federal government employees went without pay for weeks on end. They struggled to pay for basic necessities like rent and medicine, and many were expected to continue to work without pay. The Office of Personnel Management, which manages federal workers, had the audacity to suggest that furloughed workers barter for their rent in order to survive. Without essential staff to maintain some of the government's basic functions during the shutdown, some national parks were left unattended, numerous immigration cases were postponed, and security lines lengthened at airports.

What could bring on such catastrophe? The president was essentially holding the government hostage over his desire to fund the construction of a wall at the US–Mexico border, a major 2016 campaign promise and a cornerstone of his agenda against the imagined and false threat of immigrants. As soon as lawmakers reconvened in January, the House passed a set of appropriations bills that did *not* fund the wall, and Senate Majority Leader Mitch McConnell blocked them from being introduced in the Senate. When the shutdown hit its fourth week in mid-January, McConnell's silence spoke volumes, and Democrats demanded action. On January 16, Ocasio-Cortez joined a group of freshman Democrats that aimed to find McConnell to ask him to bring a Senate vote on the bills already passed in the House. Every day that the shutdown continued, more Americans suffered.

Finding McConnell, as it turned out, was absurdly difficult. "We went to his office, he wasn't there. We went to the Senate floor, and he wasn't there," tweeted Texas Representative Veronica Escobar. The group roamed the halls of Congress looking for him, hoping to confront him. Ocasio-Cortez tweeted videos of their quest. "He seems to be running away from us," Ocasio-Cortez said in the clip. "He's not in the cloakroom, he's not in the Capitol, he's not in the Russell Building, he's not on the floor of the Senate, and 800,000 people don't have their paychecks. So where's Mitch?"

The video and the hashtag #WheresMitch went viral and spawned countless memes. The moment was significant: As MSNBC anchor Lawrence O'Donnell explained on his program *The Last Word*, through her simple stunt and leverage of a hashtag, Ocasio-Cortez shifted the public discourse on the government shutdown and put pressure where it belonged—on the Senate. And she did so by simply exercising her right to walk into the Senate chamber and telegraphing the hunt. It's rare for a House member to enter the Senate chamber, O'Donnell, who formerly worked in the Senate, explained. "House members entering the Senate chamber in protest—well, that's even more rare."

Alexandria Ocasio-Cortez ✓
@AOC

800,000 workers are missing their paychecks and
we're pushing to get them paid ASAP.

We're here doing our job - the House has voted to
reopen government whole or in part several times - so
why can't we find GOP Senators to ask them do theirs?
#WheresMitch

👤 Lauren Underwood and 2 others

5:55 PM · Jan 16, 2019 · Twitter for iPhone

*Ocasio-Cortez shares a behind-the-scenes peek into the search for
Mitch McConnell in January 2019.*

Hours after she searched for McConnell, Ocasio-Cortez delivered her inaugural speech, in which she blasted Trump for the shutdown and the unbridled xenophobia that fueled his passion project at the border. "The truth of this shutdown is that it's actually not about a wall," she said. "The truth is, this shutdown is about the erosion of American democracy and the subversion of our most basic governmental norms." Overnight, the video of her nearly four-minute speech broke C-SPAN's record for most-watched Twitter video by a member of the House of Representatives.

The day's events laid to rest any lingering doubts as to whether, or how, the social media following and animated base Ocasio-Cortez had built would translate into real, actionable political power. "In modern politics—in social media politics—with fame comes power, the power to direct media attention where you want it. The power to push a policy position into the national political debate," O'Donnell said. "And Congresswoman Ocasio-Cortez did that today more effectively than any other member of the House of Representatives could have done it, because of that fame.

"We have not seen such a famous freshman member of the House," he continued, "since John Quincy Adams was elected to the House of Representatives after serving as our sixth president of the United States."

The next day she, along with Connecticut Representative Jim Himes, taught her new colleagues how to use Twitter.

★ ★ ★ ★ ★ ★ ★ ★ ★ ★ ★ ★

In politics, authenticity is a vague, elusive concept, and many who strive for it come across as anything but—especially on social media, where there's limited space or time to get a point across. In 2016, it was jarring when Hillary Clinton's social media accounts adopted the tone of a magazine for millennials. Watching former Texas Congressman Beto O'Rourke livestream his dental cleaning was awkward. As a millennial, Ocasio-Cortez is inherently more attuned to social media, but even among young people she has a special knack for it: She writes her own tweets and isn't trying to imitate someone else's voice. The most important Twitter rule for her colleagues, she told *Late Show* host Stephen Colbert, was: "Don't try to be anyone that you're not."

"Don't try to talk like a young kid if you're not a young kid. Don't post a meme if you don't know what a meme is," she said. "Don't talk like the founding fathers on Twitter. If you're a mom who likes to garden, talk like a mom that likes to garden."

When she first launched her bid for Congress, *Insider* reports that Ocasio-Cortez had fewer than 300 followers on Twitter. According to the *Guardian*, she saw a 600 percent increase in Twitter followers from June 2018 to January 2019, and one year after the primary election, she had a bigger following than Nancy Pelosi or Joe Biden: more than 4.5 million followers (over 9 million including Instagram). There's a reason why the numbers are growing: On Twitter, she's developed a reputation for clapping back against criticisms. During her popular Instagram livestreams, she riffs on current events, makes observations about Congress, and answers questions from her followers while making soup or cooking mac and cheese.

In April 2019, over 8,000 people tuned in to her hour-long livestream; in it she talked about climate change, Puerto Rico, and staying grounded while sipping on wine, eating popcorn, and assembling IKEA furniture. In one moment, she gave followers a brief history lesson on Puerto Rico, and in the next, she was distracted by the directions: "It says I need a screwdriver, which is a bad sign," she said, asking followers to comment with a thumbs-up emoji if they wanted her to continue.

The Instagram stories, which disappear within twenty-four hours unless they are pinned to her page, are an effort to "humanize our government," Ocasio-Cortez explained on MSNBC. She puts herself out there so that people watching at home can see that politics isn't, and doesn't have to be, the provenance of a group of rich white men.

Activist Wardah Khalid has called the broadcasts "the 2018 version" of President Franklin D. Roosevelt's "fireside chats," radio addresses meant to calm the nation during the 1930s and 1940s. But the idea wasn't hatched by a political consultant or communications director. Ramos Rios told an audience in 2019 that the impromptu, intimate livestreams were borne from an effort to multitask: The congresswoman had limited time, and she needed to eat and set up her DC apartment while also getting some work done. "She did not know it was going to be so big," Ramos Rios said. "This wasn't a grand plan. . . . It was literally: How do I feed myself? How do I find time to like actually talk to my constituents? And how do I do it in a way that I'd want to hear it?"

In between demystifying politics and giving pep talks, Ocasio-Cortez also responds to questions about the more mundane things

Ocasio-Cortez applies makeup on the way to an interview during her campaign.

people deal with every day, like finding beauty hacks for more manageable makeup routines. As she wrote on Twitter, "Be a fierce woman who can do both."

"Skincare is a straight up hobby of mine. I'm a science nerd, and I truly enjoy the science of it, reading about compounds and studies, etc," she wrote in one Instagram story that turned into headlines on beauty websites across the Internet. Rather than sharing specific brands and products, she outlined the important steps in her skincare routine: double cleansing, toner, serums (like retinol or Vitamin C), moisturizer, and sunscreen.

In another post, she shared her secret for picture-perfect nails: press-ons. "The trick," she wrote, "is to wait a bit and then file them down to your natural/desired shape. I usually go with plain nails but when I want a little pick me up or if an event is coming I'll grab these at the drug store. They last for a week!" She put them on at 12:39 a.m. while aboard an Amtrak train to the Capitol after a "TRAVEL DRAMA day" that included a flight delay and eventual cancellation.

Her approach to social media is incredibly simple—it's just like tuning in to a friend's feed. But that's exactly what makes Ocasio-Cortez unique: She's not your friend—she's one of the most famous lawmakers in the country.

THE "S" WORD

I n between moments of casting immigrants as criminals during his State of the Union speech in February 2019, Trump identified what he saw as a new growing danger: socialism.

"Here, in the United States, we are alarmed by new calls to adopt socialism in our country," Trump said. "Tonight, we renew our resolve that America will never be a socialist country."

Ocasio-Cortez arrives to hear Trump deliver his second State of the Union address in February 2019.

The face of that threat (to Republicans, at least) was a twenty-nine-year-old Latina who had been in Congress for only one month.

"The president spent a lot of time using the 'S' word," *Meet the Press* host Chuck Todd said to Ocasio-Cortez in an interview later that week. "I don't know whether it's a dig or an enhancement. I'll let you decide."

"I was flattered," Ocasio-Cortez said, laughing.

While Ocasio-Cortez wears Trump's endless ire like a badge of honor, his State of the Union speech illustrated the growing power that she, and the leftist democratic socialism movement she represents, wield today. More young people are embracing socialism: A 2017 YouGov poll found that 44 percent of millennials want to live in a socialist country, while only 26 percent of baby boomers would prefer socialism. According to polling by Gallup, public perception of socialism is more favorable today than it was in the 1940s.

There's a lot of misinformation about the political philosophy that Ocasio-Cortez espouses. In the early 1900s, the Socialist Party of America ran as an influential third political party, but in the 1970s, the organization collapsed as leaders disagreed about strategic visions. One of its former leaders, a political theorist and activist named Michael Harrington, went on to found a group that became the DSA. Harrington recognized that, in order to broaden socialism's influence, the movement needed to work within the two-party American political system. He sought to bring reforms from the labor, civil rights, environmental, and feminist movements into the liberal wing of the Democratic Party—what Harrington called "the left-wing of the possible." According to

Maurice Isserman, professor of history at Hamilton College, who is a charter member of the DSA and author of *The Other American: The Life of Michael Harrington,* Ocasio-Cortez "is running not as a third party, not as a socialist—she's running with Democrats in the House and in the Senate to pass legislation. It's not socialist, it's democratic socialist."

Certainly, democratic socialism is nothing like what Trump suggested it to be in his speech, which drew on 1950s-era Red Scare fears. What Bernie Sanders and Ocasio-Cortez are advocating for under their brand of democratic socialism is really a return to the New Deal programs introduced by Democratic President Franklin D. Roosevelt during the Great Depression, but greatly expanded to include racial and environmental justice. Sanders further elaborated in a 2015 speech at Georgetown University, saying it is "the right to a decent job at decent pay; the right to adequate food, clothing, and time off from work; the right for every business, large and small, to function in an atmosphere free from unfair competition and domination by monopolies; the right of all Americans to have a decent home and decent health care."

Ocasio-Cortez centered her platform on similar issues: "In a modern, moral, and wealthy society, no person in America should be too poor to live," she told Stephen Colbert the day after her primary election win. "What that means to me is health care as a human right. It means that every child, no matter where you are born, should have access to a college or trade school education if they so choose it. . . . I think that no person should be homeless if we can have public structures and public policy to allow for people to have homes and food and lead a dignified life in the United States."

(Ocasio-Cortez has pointed to Canada, Sweden, and Denmark as successful models.)

The DSA's membership was dwindling for decades, but it now has around 55,000 members (up from just 6,000 in 2015) and the demographics have changed, with the average age moving from sixty-four to thirty-three. Isserman credits Sanders for bringing democratic socialism back into public conversation, and Ocasio-Cortez for making it popular again.

Ocasio-Cortez speaks about her first few months in Congress at a South by Southwest panel in Austin, Texas.

WALKING
THE WALK

ills take time to pass, but there was one place Ocasio-Cortez could begin implementing her proposals right away: her office. In December 2018, she announced that her office would become one of the few to pay interns (at a rate of $15 per hour). "Time to walk the walk," she tweeted. "Very few members of Congress actually pay their interns. We will be one of them." (According to a 2017 study by Pay Our Interns, only 3.6 percent of House Democratic interns and 8 percent of House Republican interns are paid.)

In May 2019, she rolled out a paid parental leave policy that would cover new parents—biological or adoptive, regardless of gender—for twelve weeks. America is the only industrialized country without a federally mandated paid family leave policy, which exacerbates the gender wage gap, perpetuates gendered expectations in the office (and at home), and puts too many working people in the impossible scenario of having to choose between earning a paycheck and taking care of a loved one.

"Equal pay at work is about SO much more than the salary you offer," Ocasio-Cortez tweeted. "If you give dads less paid parental leave than moms, you're contributing to the pay gap. If you see

A colorful group of notes adorns the wall outside Ocasio-Cortez's office.

pregnancy or family as a workplace obstacle, you're contributing to the pay gap." New moms can use her personal office for pumping and feeding, and staff are encouraged to bring their babies to work. "We talk about what play mats + cribs we need along w/ our legislative agenda," she wrote.

★ ★ ★ ★ ★ ★ ★ ★ ★ ★ ★ ★

In January 2019, the congresswoman was among the high-profile freshman progressives given spots on two of the powerful House committees: the House Financial Services Committee, which, under chair and California firebrand Representative Maxine Waters, has taken aim at predatory lending practices, and the House Committee on Oversight and Reform, which plays a major role in the investigations of the Trump administration.

"Personally, I'm looking forward to digging into the student loan crisis, examining for-profit prisons/ICE detention, and exploring the development of public & postal banking. To start. ☺," she tweeted upon the announcement. In February 2019, she asked a panel of campaign finance watchdog groups about whether there were any regulations that prevented lawmakers "from being bought off by wealthy corporations." A clip of the exchange racked up more than 37 million views, breaking the record for the most-watched political video ever posted on Twitter, according to analytics company Tubular. In April, when the committee called in the heads of the big banks for the first time since 2009, she pointedly asked CEOs whether they believed more of them should be in jail. "I represent kids that go to jail for jumping a turnstile because they can't afford a MetroCard," she told JP Morgan CEO Jamie Dimon. "Do you think that more folks should have gone to jail for their role in a financial crisis that led to 7.8 million foreclosures in the 10 years between 2007 and 2016?"

Ocasio-Cortez, along with Representatives Rashida Tlaib and Ayanna Pressley, also made waves in the House Committee on Oversight and Reform, which has the power to subpoena Trump administration officials. In February 2019, the committee questioned former Trump lawyer and fixer Michael Cohen, who has pleaded guilty to a dizzying number of financial crimes. Ocasio-Cortez had some of the most incisive inquiries of the hearing, using her allotted time to ask Cohen specific questions about the people who handled Trump's insurance claims and financial assets,

Ocasio-Cortez, Pressley, and Tlaib listen as Michael Cohen testifies before the House Committee on Oversight and Reform.

entering their names in public record and thus enabling the committee to dig deeper into the president's elusive tax and financial records. Pressley and Tlaib followed up with more questions, and the most remarkable moment of their exchange was watching them call out the racism of their senior Republican colleague, Mark Meadows, a white man who took issue with calling Trump "a racist."

One after another, the women fired their questions, which, as I wrote in *Jezebel*, "were like a series of punches into a thick, unscalable wall blocking the road to progress; each on its own was significant, but taken collectively, these 15 minutes were a glimpse into the changing tides of the country."

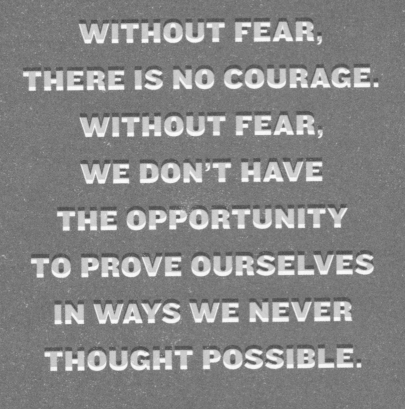

★ ★ ★ ★ ★ ★ ★ ★ ★

"

**WITHOUT FEAR,
THERE IS NO COURAGE.
WITHOUT FEAR,
WE DON'T HAVE
THE OPPORTUNITY
TO PROVE OURSELVES
IN WAYS WE NEVER
THOUGHT POSSIBLE.**

"

★ ★ ★ ★ ★ ★ ★ ★ ★

As Ocasio-Cortez maintained her outspokenness, she continued to be vulnerable in the public eye. After her first House Committee on Oversight and Reform hearing in January, she admitted in an Instagram post, "It's always intimidating to speak up in a new setting." She explained the complicated rules of speaking in Congress and wrote, "Breaking these rules can have consequences small and large: not knowing how means you could lose precious speaking time, or miss an opportunity to make a point. Opposing party members are always looking for the slightest slip-up to gum up process or make an example of you." Few of us can relate to being in Congress, but most people can relate to feeling inadequate or too intimidated to speak up.

She went on: "Here's my trick: For a long time, I've used fear as a guiding light 💡 instead of a reason to turn off. . . . But I've very frequently interpreted fear as a growth cusp. Aside from some concrete fears, we often don't know what we're afraid of until we get there, and feel it. Fear tells us how to grow. Fear, like a lot of discomfort, forces us to choose: 'Do I do this, or not?'"

REPUBLICAN OBSESSION

As popular as Ocasio-Cortez has become with a faction of the left, she has become a target on the right. Her embrace of democratic socialism and her ability to confront her peers and critics (especially as a woman of color) represent a looming existential threat to the leadership of the Republican Party.

At first, the "controversies" surrounding Ocasio-Cortez only made her more popular with progressives. The initial biography on her campaign website, perhaps tailored to tie her more closely to the district in which she was running, was technically correct but implied that her family lived in the Bronx while she commuted to another school district as a child. Republicans were scandalized when they discovered that the "girl from the Bronx" grew up in the more affluent Westchester County. In 2018, *Newsmax* host John Cardillo tweeted a Google Street View photo of Ocasio-Cortez's modest childhood home, arguing it was located in a "very nice area," and calling it "a far cry from the Bronx hood upbringing she's selling." Ocasio-Cortez snapped back on Twitter: "It is nice. Growing up, it was a good town for working people. My mom scrubbed toilets so I could live here & I grew up seeing how the zip code one is born in determines much of their opportunity. Your attempt to strip me of my family, my story, my home, and my identity is exemplary of how scared you are of the power of all four of those things."

In January 2019, a now-deleted Twitter account called AnonymousQ released a thirty-second clip of Ocasio-Cortez dancing on a rooftop of a building. "Here is America's favorite commie know-it-all acting like the clueless nitwit she is," the tweet read, saying it was a "high school video of 'Sandy' Ocasio-Cortez." In reality, the video was from Ocasio-Cortez's college years, in which she and some friends delightfully reenacted a scene from *The Breakfast Club* set to Phoenix's "Lisztomania." It immediately went viral—not for the reasons conservatives had hoped—and tripled the song's on-demand audio and video streams that week and landed the tune on YouTube's top songs list. Ocasio-Cortez got in on the joke and shared a new video of her dancing, this time as a congresswoman. In an eleven-second clip, which was viewed more than 20 million times, she lip-synched to Edwin Starr's 1970 hit "War" as she twirled in front of her new office. "I hear the GOP thinks women dancing are scandalous," she tweeted. "Wait till they find out Congresswomen dance too 💃!"

Over time, however, the obsession of some Republican officials and pundits grew deeper, more sinister, and more dangerous. According to a study by Media Matters for America, a watchdog group that monitors conservative media outlets, the Fox News Channel and its sister Fox Business Network mentioned Ocasio-Cortez 3,181 times during the six-week period from February 25 to April 7, 2019 (about seventy-six times a day). Fox

A still from the video of Ocasio-Cortez dancing with her college classmates in 2010.

News host Tucker Carlson has called her an "idiot wind bag," a "pompous little twit," a "fake revolutionary," "self-involved and dumb," and a "moron and nasty and more self-righteous than any televangelist." She has become "someone for hosts and guests to demonize, knock down and refer to whenever grievances need to be aired against the Democratic Party," Media Matters wrote.

Commentary from some Republicans, including the president, is openly racist. In July 2019, Trump tweeted that Omar, Pressley, Tlaib, and Ocasio-Cortez—four progressive women of color who routinely call out his bigotry and violent policies—should "go back" and fix the countries they "originally came from." While he said that Trump should "knock it down a notch," South Carolina Senator Lindsey Graham called the women "a bunch of communists," which draws on a deep and rich history of white people invoking communism to dismiss black activism and social change. As Ocasio-Cortez tweeted in response, the term

Ocasio-Cortez, Tlaib, Omar, and Pressley at a press conference responding to the derogatory remarks Trump posted on Twitter in July 2019.

communist "was one of the preferred smears against integrating schools, & one of the main attacks segregationists used against MLK Jr."

The commentary has also been overtly sexist: Right-wingers have simultaneously dismissed Ocasio-Cortez as a child (one Republican strategist called her "a little girl" on television) and oversexualized her, as the *Daily Caller* did when posting a now-deleted tweet that read: "Here's The Photo Some People Described As A Nude Selfie of Alexandria Ocasio-Cortez." Florida Representative Matt Gaetz told *TMZ* that he'd "swipe right"—an apparent reference to the Tinder dating app—for the chance to work with her, and has called her an "attractive lady from Queens."

Washington Examiner writer Eddie Scarry tweeted an invasive, creepy photo of the back of Ocasio-Cortez as she walked through a hallway, writing: "Hill staffer sent me this pic of Ocasio-Cortez they took just now. I'll tell you something: that jacket and coat don't look like a girl who struggles." The obsession with Ocasio-Cortez's looks and money is part of an age-old script employed by men to knock a woman down a few pegs and put her back in her place.

But Ocasio-Cortez refuses to give in to the attacks. "I think they saw a woman of color—Latina, no less—that came from a working-class and poor background, that ascended to federal office, and they said, 'We cannot allow this to have credibility, because if people saw that she did it, then maybe others will come—and we cannot let other people like her run for office. We need to make an example out of her,'" Ocasio-Cortez told *Vanity Fair* in March 2019.

She frequently claps back on Twitter—a mechanism that isn't just "reflexive self-defense," as she told Ta-Nehisi Coates in January 2019. "I'm trying to dismantle some of the frames—of misogyny, classism, racism—that we've just allowed to go on."

Ocasio-Cortez pointed out how the Republican demonization of her has also turned her into a target for violence: In July 2019, ProPublica uncovered a secret Border Patrol Facebook group in which its more than 9,000 members shared violent, racist, and misogynistic memes about migrants and politicians, including Ocasio-Cortez. In it, they "joked about the deaths of migrants, discussed throwing burritos at Latino members of Congress visiting a detention facility in Texas . . . and posted a vulgar illustration depicting Rep. Alexandria Ocasio-Cortez engaged in oral sex with a detained migrant, according to screenshots of their postings," the outlet reported.

In May 2019, a Memorial Day montage at a Fresno Grizzlies baseball game featured her photo sandwiched between that of North Korean dictator Kim Jong Un and the late Cuban dictator Fidel Castro.

"What people don't (maybe do) realize is when orgs air these hateful messages, my life changes bc of the flood of death threats they inspire," she tweeted about the incident. She wrote that she has spent several mornings drinking coffee and reviewing "photos of the men (it's always men) who want to kill me."

"I don't even get to see all of them. Just the ones that have been flagged as particularly troubling," she continued. "It happens whenever Fox gets particularly aggressive + hateful, too. Young interns have to constantly hear hateful messages (far beyond disagreement) from ppl we don't even rep."

Though the administration denies it, there is a clear connection between bigoted speech and acts of violence: Trump has called Mexicans "rapists" and "criminals," paving the way for a policy that forcibly separates migrant children from their parents. His anti-Muslim speeches created a path for his travel ban, leading to an uptick in hate crimes and Islamophobia greater than what the country saw in the aftermath of 9/11. Taking clear aim at Trump and his party, Ocasio-Cortez wrote: "All of this is to say that words matter, and can have consequences for safety. For those who believe in 'free speech': whose free speech do you believe in? Bc some folks using free speech to defend racism are also supporting folks passing laws to allow running over protesters."

The hateful rhetoric and the relentless taunts have real-life consequences. She receives so many death threats that Capitol police have trained her staff in performing risk assessments of all visitors, even ones dropping by to leave a kind note. In February 2019, a forty-nine-year-old Coast Guard lieutenant and white nationalist was charged for stockpiling guns; he was planning to attack a number of Democratic leaders, including Ocasio-Cortez.

"I miss being able to go outside in sweats," she told *Time*. "I can't go anywhere in public and just be a person without a lot of people watching everything I do."

But she is determined not to let the threats slow her down—if anything, becoming a target has emboldened her. "When you bust out that door and you're like, 'No, I'm not going to let you make me feel that way'—it's kind of jarring. It's like, 'Wait, she's not stopping, and she's supposed to stop,'" Ocasio-Cortez told *Vanity Fair*. "It can be very empowering to say, 'Make fun of me. Do it. Draw the little insults on my face. . . . Do what you're gonna do. Act more and more childish. Just do it, because you're not gonna stop. You're just not gonna stop this movement.'"

CALL ME A RADICAL

Though Ocasio-Cortez has breathed new life into the Democratic Party, some tenured Democrats are urging her to tone down her inner-party protests and learn the ropes. "I'm sure Ms. Cortez means well, but there's almost an outstanding rule: Don't attack your own people," Missouri Representative Emanuel Cleaver told *Politico*. "We just don't need sniping in our Democratic Caucus." Others are wary of her celebrity status, with one anonymous House member telling the outlet: "She needs to decide: Does she want to be an effective legislator or just continue being a Twitter star?"

The congresswoman has also made a few missteps that could hint at her inexperience: In December 2018, the *Washington Post* Fact Checker column called the congresswoman-elect out for an inaccurate tweet in which she claimed that "$21 trillion in 'Pentagon accounting errors' could have paid for 66 percent of the Medicare-for-all proposal," one of many of her claims they have rated as false. Her office also fumbled the unveiling of the Green New Deal resolution when they released a "frequently asked questions" draft that included ideas and proposals that went beyond the scope of what many Democrats had signed on to support.

The inaccuracies have undoubtedly attracted more criticism due to her fame, fueling Fox News for days on end while drawing skepticism from pundits and TV anchors. And, as *Vox*'s Laura McGann argued, Ocasio-Cortez likely faces more scrutiny as a woman of color who works in a male-dominated landscape.

In an interview on *60 Minutes* in January 2019, Anderson Cooper asked her to respond to criticism that her "math is fuzzy," specifically referencing the Pentagon statistics. "If people want to really blow up one figure here or one word there, I would argue that they're missing the forest for the trees," she said in response. "I think that there's a lot of people more concerned about being precisely, factually, and semantically correct than about being morally right." Both Ocasio-Cortez and Cooper raised fair points: Facts, of course, *do* matter, and as a politician, Ocasio-Cortez should expect to be held accountable for her statements. But she is also right to point out that, in an age when the president routinely uses racist, transphobic, and sexist lies to justify violence and oppression, the intent behind a falsehood and the impact it has are relevant context for the media to consider.

Another major criticism of Ocasio-Cortez is that her grand social projects are too "pie in the sky"—impossible to succeed in a divided Congress, and far too costly for the government and taxpayers. Some estimates say her programs, if enacted, would cost more than $40 trillion over the next decade. She has proposed taxing the ultrarich to pay for the programs, but critics point out that won't foot the whole bill. When confronted with that reality, Ocasio-Cortez pivoted back to her ideological argument. After Cooper expressed skepticism of the Green New Deal, she said, "No one asks how we're going to pay for this Space Force. No one asked how we paid for a two-trillion-dollar tax cut. We only ask how we pay for it on issues of housing, health care, and education." Taking on such ambitious initiatives, she explained in an interview with CNN's Jake Tapper, requires a total government reprioritization: "They're not short-term Band-Aids, but they are really profound decisions about who we want to be as a nation and . . . how we want to act, as the wealthiest nation in the history of the world."

Ocasio-Cortez's power is not so much in brokering legislative deals, but in reimagining what's possible and resetting an agenda for Democrats. Responding to criticism that her ideas are too "out there," she told Cooper, "I think that it's only ever been radicals that have changed this country. Abraham Lincoln made the radical decision to sign the Emancipation Proclamation. Franklin Delano Roosevelt made the *radical* decision to embark on establishing programs like Social Security. That is *radical*." When Cooper asked if she considered herself a radical, she said, "Yeah, you know, if that's what radical means, call me a radical."

★ ★ ★ ★ ★ ★ ★ ★ ★ ★ ★

Ocasio-Cortez's radicalism has made her popular with activists, but across the spectrum, she represents a minority of voters. In mid-February 2019, Amazon canceled its highly controversial plan for a sprawling second headquarters in Long Island City, Queens. Many Democrats, including New York Governor Andrew Cuomo and Mayor Bill de Blasio, welcomed Amazon and the white-collar jobs it would bring to the state. Long Island City sits just outside of Ocasio-Cortez's district, but the congresswoman became one of the most vocal—and certainly the most high-profile—politicians opposed to the campus, arguing that it would displace low-income people and exacerbate income inequality.

According to a Siena College Research Institute survey of 700 voters, a majority of respondents across the state supported the move, and when it fell through, nearly 40 percent blamed Ocasio-Cortez. The polling suggested that in New York, "the progressive base that cheered Ms. Ocasio-Cortez as she railed against the deal was not representative of most voters," the *New York Times* wrote. The public's perception of Ocasio-Cortez's role in the Amazon debacle illustrated the power of her endorsement and her polarizing influence in politics. As a New York lobbyist told *Politico,* "Anytime I talk to someone—companies, corporations looking to do business in New York, nonprofits rolling out an issue campaign, the first question they always ask me is 'Where is AOC on this?'"

Many Democratic leaders have argued that Ocasio-Cortez, who came in with the energy and idealism of an activist, does not represent a winning strategy in areas beyond New York City's liberal bubble. Nancy Pelosi has repeatedly dismissed the notion that her brand of progressivism is the future of the party, writing off Tlaib, Pressley, Omar, and Ocasio-Cortez in a *New York Times* interview as "four people" with "their public whatever and their Twitter world." During a visit to the UK in April 2019, Pelosi said, "When we won this election, it wasn't in districts like mine or Alexandria's." Picking up a glass of water at the table, she added, "Those are districts that are solidly Democratic. This glass of water would win with a D next to its name in those districts."

Former Democratic vice presidential candidate Joe Lieberman, who now identifies as an independent, told Fox Business News in early 2019, "I certainly hope [Ocasio-Cortez is] not the future and I don't believe she is," saying she was too far-left. "If you look at the majority of new Democrats in the House, they tend to be, I say, center-left, if they are not left-left. And that is because they had to be center-left to win some of those competitive swing districts that they took from Republicans."

While Ocasio-Cortez's democratic socialist views certainly don't appeal to everyone, to dismiss her election as a fluke or as something that cannot be replicated in another district is to ignore the change that is happening across the country: A 2019 survey by CNBC found that a majority of Americans support Medicare for all, tuition-free college, and government-funded childcare. The protests around the Green New Deal turned climate change into a leading issue for Democrats in the 2020 election, and activists succeeded in getting more than a dozen presidential candidates to promise not to accept money from the fossil fuel industry. John Della Volpe, who analyzes shifts in political attitudes at the Harvard Kennedy School Institute of Politics, told *Time* that "Every year, young people are ticking a couple points more left."

For now, Ocasio-Cortez claims to be unfazed by the criticism of her peers. "I want to ask this question in a respectful manner, knowing also that you're from Queens, so you will understand this question," Stephen Colbert said, referencing the flak she's caught from fellow Democrats who want her to wait her turn. "On a scale from zero to some, how many fucks do you give?"

Ocasio-Cortez replied, "I think it's zero."

MOVING LEFT

In what felt like a rebuke to Trump and his policies, Congress ushered in its most diverse group of elected officials ever in 2018, with Ocasio-Cortez arguably becoming the most famous. She has created an army of followers on social media, wielding the power and charisma more akin to a pop star than a politician, and she has become an icon for the progressive movement. In a *Jezebel* post about the women who inspired us in 2018, I wrote about Ocasio-Cortez and her squad: "Together, they have infused a new energy into politics and are challenging the Democratic Party to move further left; to define itself not just in opposition to Trump, but to stand up for a new set of values and priorities that places women of color, LGBTQ people, and immigrants at the forefront." Her election represents the most successful test case of a new political strategy for the left: to play offense, not defense. "There's this really myopic and just . . . misunderstanding of politics as this flat, two-dimensional, left-right thing," Ocasio-Cortez explained on *Pod Save America*. "So they always feel like, 'Okay, the right says this thing, we have to respond to it!' That's why [the right is] winning. That's why they've won for the last ten years; because they've dragged us onto their court. And we've refused to have our own strong message to force them to play defense on."

THE
PHENOM

How **Alexandria
Ocasio-Cortez**
became America's
lightning rod
*By CHARLOTTE
ALTER*

CHANGING
THE CLIMATE
FIGHT
*By JUSTIN
WORLAND*

The April 2019 cover of Time,
featuring Ocasio-Cortez.

In the years to come, the question that remains is: Will the progressive, activist-driven base that Ocasio-Cortez champions emerge as the future of the Democratic Party, or will her supporters continue to be a vocal minority that party leaders work to keep at bay? Regardless, one thing is certain: She has captured the attention of millions and inspired a generation of young people.

In April 2019, just three months after she came into office, Ocasio-Cortez landed on the cover of *Time*—a rare distinction for a freshman in Congress. Later that month, the magazine named Ocasio-Cortez one of the 100 Most Influential People in the World. Massachusetts Senator Elizabeth Warren, one of the nation's leading progressives who had announced her 2020 presidential bid just months before, penned the honorific:

Her commitment to putting power in the hands of the people is forged in fire. Coming from a family in crisis and graduating from school with a mountain of debt, she fought back against a rigged system and emerged as a fearless leader in a movement committed to demonstrating what an economy, a planet and a government that works for everyone should look like. A year ago, she was taking orders across a bar. Today, millions are taking cues from her. She reminds all of us that even while greed and corruption slow our progress, even while armies of lobbyists swarm Washington, in our democracy, true power still rests with the people. And she's just getting started.

"She can shape media cycles in a way that nobody on the left has been able to do since the advent of cable, really," Ryan Grim told me. "That allows her to set the agenda in a way."

Ta-Nehisi Coates, who famously made the case for reparations in an *Atlantic* cover story in 2014, has said that the congresswoman embodies Martin Luther King Jr.'s "radical vision."

Political analysts are already debating whether or not she will run for president one day. But Ocasio-Cortez told Coates in January 2019 that she's not looking to run for another position any time soon—and that's part of why she can be so bold. "I think the reason why I'm able and why I choose to speak the way that I choose to speak, in a way that some people would say is risky, is because I don't attach myself to some kind of ambition or vision of myself for the future," she said. "I think it is exactly that behavior that prevents people from speaking truth to power today."

Despite her meteoric rise into the nation's consciousness as a symbol of hope to Gen Y and a villain to Republicans, Ocasio-Cortez insists that she's still the same woman from the Bronx who saw injustices that she wanted to fix. "It's really hard to communicate that I'm just a normal person doing her best," she told *Vanity Fair.* "I'm not a superhero. I'm not a villain. I'm just a person that's trying."

Abolish ICE

When former President George W. Bush signed bipartisan legislation to create the Department of Homeland Security (DHS) in 2002, he said its underlying mission was to "protect our citizens against the dangers of a new era" in the wake of 9/11. In reality, the creation of DHS—a gargantuan department that absorbed twenty-two federal agencies—was a reactionary move that recharacterized immigrants as potential national security threats. Under DHS's oversight, Immigration and Customs Enforcement (ICE) runs a massive network of detention centers that have become another tool in America's expanding deportation machine.

Activists, particularly in immigrant communities, have been calling out the abuses of ICE since its inception, but under the Trump administration, ICE's inhumane and cruel treatment of migrants has prompted a national outcry. Ocasio-Cortez amplified the message, making the abolition of ICE a major proposal in her campaign. "I think what the abolition of ICE means to me is, first and foremost, we have to respect the inalienable rights of all people, including migrants. We have to end family detention and we have end the practice of incarcerating children . . . we need to end private prisons and private detention centers, which is largely under ICE's purview," Ocasio-Cortez told *Business Insider*.

In July 2019, she visited detention centers along the southern border. During an emotional House Committee on Oversight and Reform hearing about the conditions at DHS–run centers, she said, "That children were being separated from their parents in front of an American flag . . . we cannot allow for this."

Green New Deal

According to a recent report by the United Nations, the world has only twelve years to stave off extreme, wide-scale environmental disasters like famine, disease, and displacement. Instead of taking action, however, the Trump administration rolled back regulations that protect the environment. The Green New Deal is an ambitious, activist-led agenda to move the United States to 100 percent renewable energy, invest in communities of color that have been disproportionately affected by environmental disaster, and eliminate greenhouse gas emissions—all before that twelve-year deadline.

Ocasio-Cortez adopted the Green New Deal, which she introduced as a resolution with Senator Edward Markey, as part of her congressional platform. The repeated protests by the Sunrise Movement, which she joined, helped turn the package into a major debate topic among Democrats running in the 2020 presidential election. Ocasio-Cortez realizes how ambitious the proposal is, but says it's what's required to prevent an unprecedented catastrophe. "It's going to require a lot of rapid change that we don't even conceive of as possible right now," she told Anderson Cooper on *60 Minutes*. "What is the problem with trying to push our technological capacities to the furthest extent possible?"

Medicare for All

According to a 2019 study from the Johns Hopkins Bloomberg School of Public Health, on average, Americans spend much more for health care, but receive less of it, than people in other wealthy countries. This has created a bleak, untenable reality: About 40 percent of Americans are only one emergency away from financial collapse, according a 2019 report by Prosperity Now, a national nonprofit that aims to increase economic opportunity for low-income families. (That rate is even higher for black and Latinx families, who have significantly smaller financial cushions than white families.)

Medicare for all would be a single-payer, government-run health care program that would expand the current Medicare program—which covers only senior citizens, people with disabilities, and people suffering from permanent kidney failure—to cover all Americans. At various points throughout American history, politicians on both sides of the aisle have pushed for universal health care, and thanks to progressives like Sanders and Ocasio-Cortez, who have made it a central part of their platforms, the idea is making a comeback. A 2019 poll by the nonpartisan Kaiser Family Foundation found that there's been a 16 percent increase in support for the idea since 1998, and six in ten Americans now "favor a national health plan or Medicare-for-all plan."

"In my on-boarding to Congress, I get to pick my insurance plan. As a waitress, I had to pay more than TWICE what I'd pay as a member of Congress," Ocasio-Cortez tweeted weeks before being sworn into office. "It's frustrating that Congressmembers would deny other people affordability that they themselves enjoy. Time for #MedicareForAll."

Federal Jobs Guarantee

The idea of a federal jobs guarantee is simple: Everyone is entitled to a job with a living wage as a basic right. The concept was included as part of the Green New Deal resolution, which Ocasio-Cortez introduced in the House, and covers the right to "a job with a family-sustaining wage, adequate family and medical leave, paid vacations, and retirement security to all people of the United States." A federal jobs guarantee lifts everyone up, and it would especially help women of color, who are far more likely to be paid poverty-level wages than white people.

Though it's a bold proposal for Congress, it's not an altogether new idea—civil rights leaders like Martin Luther King Jr. called for a federal jobs guarantee. He said in a 1965 interview, "We must develop a federal program of public works, retraining, and jobs for all—so that none, white or black, will have cause to feel threatened. At the present time, thousands of jobs a week are disappearing in the wake of automation and other production efficiency techniques."

The roadblocks to such a plan are obvious: There are many critics, on both sides of the aisle, who argue the program would be a logistical nightmare and the costs prohibitive. But the idea is gaining traction among Democrats, and most Americans support it. Several cost estimates for the plan put it at a fraction of Trump's proposed tax cuts. Creating jobs for working-class people, Ocasio-Cortez argues, is a better use of government funds than making the ultrarich richer.

Free Public College

Ocasio-Cortez is one of the nearly 45 million Americans saddled with student loan debt. She made free public college tuition a central position in her campaign, and in June 2019, she supported the College for All Act, legislation sponsored by Minnesota Representative Ilhan Omar, Washington Representative Pramila Jayapal, and Senator Bernie Sanders, which aims to eliminate the $1.6 trillion in student debt burden for all Americans.

At a press conference about the bill, Ocasio-Cortez told reporters, "A year ago, I was waiting tables in a restaurant, and it was literally easier for me to become the youngest woman in American history elected to Congress than it is to pay off my student loan debt.

"That should tell you everything about the state of our economy and the state of quality of life for working people, because in order for me to get a chance to have health care, in order for me to get a chance to pay off my student loans, I had to do something that was nearly impossible," she said. It shouldn't take being elected to Congress "to access education, health care, and a bevy of other things that should be considered human rights."

SOURCE LIST

The sources below proved to be especially helpful in the writing of this book. For the extended bibliography, visit workman.com/AOC.

Author Interviews: Queens DSA field organizer Aaron Taube, Ocasio-Cortez volunteer Ethan Felder, National Hispanic Institute's Lorenzo De Zavala Youth Legislative Session director Julio Cotto, Cornell University history professor Lawrence Glickman, Tandem cofounder Scott Starrett, *We've Got People* author Ryan Grim, Ocasio-Cortez campaign manager Virginia Ramos Rios, Brand New Congress communications director Zeynab Day, Justice Democrats executive director Alexandra Rojas, political strategist Monica Klein, Hamilton College history professor Maurice Isserman, Georgetown University professor Michael Kazin.

60 Minutes. "Alexandria Ocasio-Cortez: The Rookie Congresswoman Challenging the Democratic Establishment." • Cadigan, Hilary. "Alexandra Ocasio-Cortez Learned Her Most Important Lessons from Restaurants." *Bon Appétit*, November 7, 2018. • Chávez, Aída, and Ryan Grim. "A Primary Against the Machine: A Bronx Activist Looks to Dethrone Joseph Crowley, the King of Queens." *The Intercept*, May 22, 2018. • Dao, James. "Manton Plans to Retire from Congress at End of Year." *The New York Times*, July 22, 1998 • Duarte, Barbara Corbellini and Nisha Stickles. "Exclusive: Alexandria Ocasio-Cortez explains what democratic socialism means to her." *Business Insider*, March 4, 2019. • Ferré-Sadurní, Luis, Andy Newman, and Vivian Wang. "Alexandria Ocasio-Cortez Emerges as a Political Star." *The New York Times*, June 27, 2018 • Gould, Jessica. "The Man Running Against Alexandria Ocasio-Cortez." *WNYC*, September 25, 2018 • Grim, Ryan. *We've Got People: From Jesse Jackson to AOC, the End of Big Money and the Rise of a Movement.* Strong Arm Press, 2019. • Lambiet, Jose. "Alexandria Ocasio-Cortez's Mother Tells How She Hopes Her Daughter Marries Her Longtime Boyfriend." *Daily Mail Online*, March 5, 2019. • *The Late Show with Stephen Colbert.* "Alexandria Ocasio-Cortez: Trump Isn't Ready for a Girl from the Bronx." • Lears, Rachel, dir. *Knock Down the House.* US: Netflix, 2019. • Ocasio-Cortez, Alexandria Facebook, Instagram, Twitter • Ocasio-Cortez, Alexandria. "An Interview with Alexandria Ocasio-Cortez, the Young Democratic Socialist Who Just Shocked the Establishment." Interview by Jeremy Scahill. *The Intercept*, June 27, 2018. • *Pod Save America.* "Alexandria Ocasio-Cortez full interview | Pod Save America." YouTube video, August 6, 2018. • Ramos Rios, Virginia, "Go Left" conference in Antwerp, Belgium, February 2019 • Relman, Eliza. "The Truth About Alexandria Ocasio-Cortez: The Inside Story of How in One Year, Sandy the Bartender Became a Lawmaker Who Triggers Both Parties." *Insider*, January 6, 2019. • Remnick, David. "Alexandria Ocasio-Cortez's Historic Win and the Future of the Democratic Party." *The New Yorker*, July 16, 2018. • The Riverside Church, *#MLKNow* 2019 by Blackout for Human Rights. • Segers, Grace. "How Alexandria Ocasio-Cortez won the race that shocked the country." *City & State NY*, June 27, 2018 • Tracy, Abigail. "'I Felt Like I Was Being Physically Ripped Apart': Alexandria Ocasio-Cortez Opens Up About Her New Fame, Trump, and Life in the Bubble." *Vanity Fair*, March 11, 2019.

CREDITS

ACKNOWLEDGMENTS

This book would not exist without the valuable contributions, advice, and support from my editor, Rachael Mt. Pleasant, and my agent, Monika Verma, who have been a dream to work with. The team at Workman has been a true force, including Susan Bolotin, Sarah Smith, Claire McKean, Beth Levy, Martha Cipolla, Zoe Maffitt, Mary Louise Mooney, Moraima Suarez, Vivian Wick, Anne Wright, Barbara Peragine, Doug Wolff, Diana Griffin, Rebecca Carlisle, and Moira Kerrigan. I would also like to acknowledge my former editors and colleagues at *Jezebel*, especially Julianne Escobedo Shepherd, whose support and edits on this project have been invaluable. To Melissa Mark Viverito, Lloyd Ultan, Monica Klein, Michael Kazin, Lawrence Glickman, Ryan Grim, Julio Cotto, Alexandra Rojas, Zeynab Day, Maurice Isserman, Virginia "Vigie" Ramos Rios, Ethan Felder, Scott Starrett, Mia Arreguin, and Aaron Taube: Thank you for sharing your invaluable insight and experiences with me.

On a more personal note, thank you to Reka Prasad for helping me navigate my career path and find my voice. To my Dadaji Sudhakar Gupta, a patron of the arts, king of his domain, and true man of leisure. I am incredibly grateful for my Buaji Aparna Kumar and Fufaji Anand Kumar, along with my cousin-siblings, who have shown me what unconditional love and support look like. To friends Marin Cogan for reading my manuscript and offering candid feedback and Rashi Rohatgi for always knowing what to say and do, even from afar. And of course, thank you to my partner Dan Sprock, who knows how to set my mind at ease and who remains my number one fan (the feeling is very mutual).

ABOUT THE AUTHOR

PRACHI GUPTA is a Brooklyn-based freelance writer and artist. Formerly, she was a senior reporter at *Jezebel* and cohost of *Jezebel*'s politics podcast, *Big Time Dicks*. She covered the 2016 election for Cosmopolitan.com, where she interviewed public figures including Ivanka Trump, Hillary Clinton, and Michelle Obama, and reported on the refugee crisis in the Middle East. She has also offered commentary for programs and documentaries on NPR, CNBC, and the UK's Channel 4, and was once called a "non-intelligent reporter" by Donald Trump. She graduated from the University of Pittsburgh in 2009.